CEM OZGUVEN

HUMAN MINDED CARE

A PATHWAY TO YOUR CUSTOMER'S HEART

OZGUVEN

Table of Contents

About the Author 5

Introduction 7

CHAPTER 1
Customers & Customer Buzzwords 11

CHAPTER 2
Human-Minded Care 25

CHAPTER 3
The Changing Role of Customers & Customer Care 35

CHAPTER 4
Care in Everything We Do 67

CHAPTER 5
Care Along the Customer Lifecycle 111

CHAPTER 6
Care Channels 159

CHAPTER 7
Performance Management 175

CHAPTER 8
Contact Centers of the Future 201

Conclusion 215

References 217

ABOUT THE AUTHOR

Cem is a human, not a supernatural creature like some thought leaders or trendsetters. He has two eyes and two ears, like any human being; maybe what makes him a little edgy is that he likes to observe the flow of events and to explore what lays beneath them.

Despite being an engineer by training, the consumer space has been his key area of interest. He wrote a post-graduate dissertation on the analysis of demand dynamics and pricing policies in consumer industries. More importantly, he is a veteran consumer, with more than 40 years of experience in consuming the products of the world.

Cem started his career as a management consultant in one of the Big Three. He later joined one of the largest companies in the consumer space and held global positions of increasing responsibility for fifteen years. Cem is a corporate entrepreneur with a history of building up businesses and organizations from scratch. He established a global e-commerce business, spanning 40 countries, and grew the annual turnover to scale – from zero. He set up a global customer care organization – people, processes and infrastructure – from scratch. His track record was proven by the satisfaction ratings of the millions of customers served. He launched direct marketing and loyalty marketing programs, winning millions of customers at different stages of the lifecycle. He also deployed a physical and digital direct-to-consumer infrastructure at a global level, handling millions of consumer interactions.

Then? He wrote this book. Why? Because while doing all the things he has done and achieving the somewhat impossible (that is to say, building direct-to-consumer practice with his bare hands in a century-old, global enterprise), he also made plenty of mistakes. And he could have done many things much better – with hindsight. So, this is the calculus of the hindsight for interested readers: an attempt to do better next time.

INTRODUCTION

The first sentence in a book usually defines what the book is about. I will take a different approach and highlight what this book is *not* about from the get-go. This book is not about customer service, call centers or issue firefighting. There are many books out there on these topics. This book is about taking care of your customers in everything you do as a business. This book is about aspiring to have your customer walk away happy from every interaction they have with your business. This book is about building a rapport with your customers that makes them want to stay with your business or even to bring their acquaintances to your business.

This may all sound like marketing a dream. Stay with me for a moment, if you will, because I have an unconventional approach and some surprising ideas about care which may convince you. For too long, care in the context of businesses providing for their customers has had it all wrong. Care has been viewed as being synonymous with customer service, and that, in turn, has been seen as a primarily reflexive activity – handling problems and calming frustrations in the face of a customer experiencing an issue. As we're going to discuss at length in this book, this aspect of care is only part of the picture, and something that all companies should work hard to avoid (but do well if necessary). In other words, the service part of care should only come late, if at all, in the customer experience. If you really care for your customers and act with their interests truly in mind, then there will be no need to provide service later because you will have already provided everything that they may need. In other words, the more you care, the less you need to service your customers. Counterintuitive, no?

I propose that we adopt a broader definition of care and approach it not as a reaction to an issue; we should instead see it as the responsibility that each company has to identify the needs of a customer, offer a solution to those needs, and provide a seamless and uncomplicated experience. This implies devising products, organization, processes and infrastructure that make the customer's life easier and more pleasant. Think about care as you would about a dinner party. When you're the host, you do everything you can to make your guest comfortable, right? You invite them in, take their coats, offer them a drink, have a pleasant chat and then do everything in your power to give your friends an enjoyable evening. Care in business should not be different than taking care of your friends or other people.

Accordingly, we define human-minded care as an approach that puts the quality of the human experience at the core of every customer interaction. Its aim is to provide what is essential to the human body, mind and soul, through the medium of your company and the products you offer.

Through this lens, we will view care as perhaps the most essential element in getting your business to gain and keep customer attention and traction. Although it is tempting to try to award that title to marketing, we must remember that marketing is only the promise, whereas care is the delivery. Care is the new marketing because, given the increased transparency and connectivity of the 21st century, your delivery is your promise; people talk about your delivery and they talk more than ever before. People trust this chatter much more than what you say about your products.

Throughout the following chapters, we are going to redefine care and finally give it the attention it deserves as a serious part of your business success. We're going to discuss in depth what human-minded care really looks like and how to develop a culture of caring within a business. We will feature both theoretical reasoning that lays the foundation to our approach and practical examples that could help you reap some quick benefits. We'll explore how customer expectations and the landscape of customer care have changed over the last decade, how it is expected to change in the future, and how to prepare for those changes and make positive use of them. We will take a look at some companies that are doing better in terms of the human-minded care approach (as well as some others that are clearly lagging behind) and will find that building trust is one of the major drivers behind this kind of philosophy. And of course, we will get into some details regarding how to track your progress and find out how our actions positively or negatively influence your customers and their affection toward your brand. I hope you will find some valuable insights here, which will not only help your customers have a better experience but also help you to better build your human-minded brand.

CHAPTER 1

Customers & Customer Buzzwords

We will explore the fundamentals of modern customer care throughout this book. However, it probably makes sense to spend some time looking into the relevant terminology first. We will start with the three most frequently used words in this book, namely "product," "brand" and "customer," and define them in a way that best serves the context of this book. We will also clarify the meanings of a list of customer-related buzz words (customer journey, customer experience, customer lifecycle, customer touchpoints, customer channels, customer episodes, customer relationship management). Interested readers presumably come across a variety of customer buzzwords in every business article they read. These buzzwords are both misused and overused, resulting in confusion and loss of meaning. It does not mean that they are useless; if used properly, they will help us conceptualize the flow of our interactions with customers.

As a word of caution, I should note that this chapter is rich in definitions and theoretical explanations. However, I believe that patiently reading this chapter is worth the time and effort as, at the end, you will have a clear understanding on how popular catchphrases tie together and be ready for the discussions in the following chapters.

A product is a solution to a consumer need or want

A "product" is any solution made available to address consumer wants or needs. Products can be goods or services; they can be tangible or intangible, such as contractual or digital products. In this book, we focus solely on consumer products, intended for the use of individuals. Industrial products (i.e. goods or services offered for the use of businesses) and industrial customers (i.e. one business supplying to another business) are out of our scope.

Eliminating the artificial distinction between goods and services by means of a broad definition is practical, especially considering that a product is, almost always, a mix of goods and services. For instance, services accompany goods sold: e.g. helpline support for a household appliance. Likewise, goods could be an element of a service delivery: e.g. retainers used to treat orthodontic problems. One good example for blurred boundaries between goods and services is dining. If you go to McDonalds and eat your Big Mac at the restaurant, you buy a service. If you go to the same McDonalds for a takeout and eat your Big Mac at home, you buy a good. The hamburger is the same, but the overall experience is different. We will get back to this point at a later stage. For the time being, the only thing to keep in mind is that anything made available to address consumer wants or needs is called a product, regardless of its goods or service nature.

We can simply define a product on two levels: basic and expanded. The basic product covers the designed functionalities, features and performance: that is to say, how well the product delivers its intended benefits (i.e. product quality in a broader sense). The expanded product covers the differentiating factors: mainly, the branding and accompanying services. Some product elements could have dual roles. For instance, the packaging necessary for protection and preservation purposes is part of the basic product whereas the packaging beyond necessity (branding) is part of the expanded product.

Let's look at the simple example of getting a haircut. The basic product, which is a service, is the hairdresser cutting your hair according to the style you would like. The resemblance of your haircut to the style you described defines the product quality. If the hairdresser suggests a style that would suit you better, that is an accompanying service (style counseling) and an element of the expanded product: an additional service accompanying the basic product. If she offers you eucalyptus drops during cold winter days or, knowing that you are on a diet, offers you a sugar-free eucalyptus drop, that is beyond the expected service. Could we call this service with a personal touch? I think so.

From here onwards, we will refer to "service product" as "product" and "accompanying service" as "service"

As the term "brand" is frequently used as a synonym to product, we will revisit its ever-evolving definition in order to avoid any ambiguity. The present-day definition of brand is the sum of all communication elements that render your product distinctive and differentiate it from all other products on the market. These elements may include the name, logo, tagline, design cues, positioning, promise and awareness. We can also define a brand as the sum of all intangible constituents which create a certain perception about your product in the customers' minds.

A brand defines what your product stands for and what kind of experience it promises to its customers. Therefore, whenever we talk about customer experience and its building blocks in this book, we will be using the term "brand" instead of product.

A customer is a regular with your business

It is worthwhile to revisit the origins of the word "customer" without getting lost in a bottomless philosophical discussion. Customer comes from the word custom, a word of Latin origin, which refers to something one repeatedly does. It suggests an established, long lasting relationship. A customer is someone who regularly deals with a business. "Consumer" is a word that is often used interchangeably with customer despite the crucial differences between the two. Consumer comes from the word consume: the act of destroying by use. The destructive nature of use suggests a temporary, unestablished relationship. The table below summarizes the key differences between a customer and a consumer for a business.

Table 1. Comparison of Customer versus Consumer

	Customer	Consumer
Origin	Custom	Consume
Related words	Customary, Customize, Custom-made	Consumable, Consumerism, Consumption
Characteristics	Individuals with distinct identities (names, addresses, likes, preferences, specific needs as well as a history of interactions and purchases)	A large group of individuals with no distinctive identities, but with some level of similarities among each other in terms of likes, preferences and needs
Business relationship	Established, long lasting (sometimes governed by a contract)	Not firmed up, changeable
Loyalty	Switching to another product involves costs (more frequently implicit, than direct costs)	Switching from one product to another could happen at any given purchase

In practice, it is assumed that the characteristics of the product define whether the users of a product are called customers or consumers: that is to say, consumer for consumable goods, customers for services and durable goods. That is true in the sense that there is a strong correlation between a business knowing the end user of its product and the product characteristics. As services and durable goods are intended for the exclusive use of a specific individual, the seller usually possesses the knowledge of the end user. It is important to note the use of "consumer" in lieu of "private individual" in some business areas, such as consumer electronics (home electronics) or consumer banking (retail banking). This use is idiomatic, as the end user possesses the characteristics of a customer.

For the same basic product, a person could be a consumer for one business and a customer for the other. Expanded product creates the difference. Let's look at a practical example. You may go to a convenience store and buy Nestlé's Mövenpick branded vanilla ice cream or go to the ice cream shop in your neighborhood and buy two scoops of vanilla ice cream (which could also be manufactured by Nestlé). It is ultimately the same basic product: vanilla ice cream, a fast-moving consumer good. However, for Nestlé, you are a consumer whereas for the local ice cream shop, you are a customer. The difference is that in one case (packaged vanilla ice cream), the product owner does not know the identity of the end user whereas in the other (two scoops of vanilla ice cream), the product owner knows who is consuming it. Knowing the end user of the product obviously leads to opportunities to customize and improve the experience (such as adding chocolate sauce and chopped pieces of walnut to the ice cream, depending on the preferences of the customer). It is easier for the local ice cream shop to establish a closer relationship with his customer.

Would it be possible for a multinational food conglomerate, whose products are consumed daily by millions of people around the world, to establish a similar relationship? The answer depends on the extent a business is able to treat its consumers like customers, in terms of knowing and addressing their individual needs and preferences. We will talk about this in length throughout the book. We will also use the terms "customer" and "consumer" (in the sense of "private individual") interchangeably, while keeping in mind the crucial difference between the two: the granularity of your knowledge about the identity and profile of the end user of your product.

Customer Experience is the accumulation of feelings

Completing the review of the basic terminology, we can now start clarifying the meanings of a list of customer-related buzz words. Customer Experience is the sum of feelings and impressions developed by a customer based on all the interactions she has had with your product, starting from the moment she discovered it. Here, it is important to remember that we are referring to the expanded product concept, which includes branding aspects. The discovery could start with hearing about the brand or product name before actually knowing anything about the basic product and its benefits. Every company delivers customer experience. Some deliver it better than others, and every interaction contributes to building the overall experience.

Customer Journey is a path

Customer Journey is the totality of the interactions in which a customer engages with your brand. In other words, it is the path the customer walks from the moment he enters into the world of your brand. Customer journey is one of the most used terms – this overuse depreciates its value. In many companies, it is treated like a godsend and people worship the concept without even understanding what it truly means. People sit in featureless meeting rooms and draw flow charts of hypotheticals, describing some ideal customer that would inexplicably roar through a bunch of channels with an endless drive to interact with the brand. I will tell you right away: that ideal customer doesn't exist. I am a firm believer in the school of thought that there are as many customer journeys as there are customers.

Customer Channel is a means

Customer Channel is the means through which customers and brands interact with each other. We can organize the channels broadly into two categories: interactive (two-way conversation) and passive (exposure to informational content). Moreover, the interaction can take place face-to-face (F2F) or remotely. The table below categorizes the channels based on interactivity, as well as the nature of the platform (traditional versus digital).

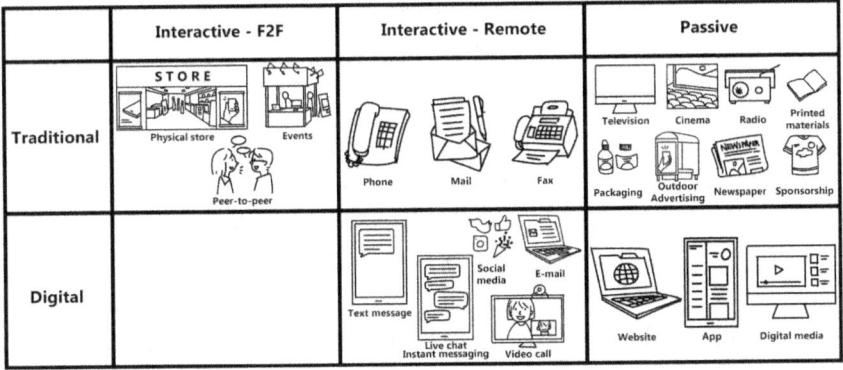

	Interactive - F2F	Interactive - Remote	Passive
Traditional	STORE — Physical store, Events, Peer-to-peer	Phone, Mail, Fax	Television, Cinema, Radio, Printed materials, Packaging, Outdoor Advertising, Newspaper, Sponsorship
Digital		Text message, Social media, E-mail, Live chat, Instant messaging, Video call	Website, App, Digital media

Some channels are paid for and fully controlled by the businesses whereas other channels might only be earned or influenced to some extent. Resultantly, no business can control the customer experience end-to-end. Under these circumstances, the proper use of a customer journey is to define the most important experience blocks for your product, identifying the most suitable channels for these (with certain fallback options) and guiding customers towards these channels in an invisible manner. In the ideal scenario, customers intuitively move to the next touchpoint with or without your explicit direction, primarily as a result of your ingenious design of the events. The name of the game is to offer customers sufficient options and facilitate their conversion into "happy users, militant promoters" (or evangelists). We will park the channel discussion here and pick it up in depth in a later chapter.

Customer Lifecycle is a progression

Customer Lifecycle refers to the progression of customers through different stages of their relationship with a product, starting from realizing the need, moving towards purchasing the product, using the product and eventually sharing their experiences with others. The typical customer lifecycle is depicted above.

Customer Touchpoint is any point in the journey
when a customer touches your brand

Customer Touchpoint is any interaction between the brand and the customer; it is a given moment in the customer lifecycle. A customer journey is composed of a series of touchpoints (moments), where each touchpoint defines the details of a specific interaction. A touchpoint emerges as a result of a specific customer need and can be defined as the combination of a channel and activity. Many touchpoints might take place in a given channel. For instance, your website is a channel. Browsing product information on your website is one touchpoint and buying a product online is another. Alternatively, the same activity could take place in two different channels – for instance, buying a product online or at a store. Touchpoints should be designed and executed in a coherent and consistent manner; they should be orchestrated to collectively deliver the desired experience blocks.

CRM powers customer interactions

Customer Relationship Management (CRM) refers to the strategy used by companies to manage direct sales and service interactions with their current and potential customers. It involves recording and analyzing customer data (such as personal information, preferences, purchase history, service history, etc.) throughout the customer lifecycle with the aim of selecting the right course of action for each customer and personalizing future interactions. However, in practice, CRM is frequently used as a synonym for the technology used to record and analyze the CRM data. CRM is the engine that powers all interactions with the customers.

Customer Episode is a chapter in the journey

Customer Episode is a series of interactions between the customer and your brand. They are triggered by the realization of a need and end with the fulfillment of that need. For instance,

- Consider the following episode: "I want to buy a product that satisfies my needs." This episode may involve touchpoints, such as searching for alternative products online, asking for advice from friends, visiting a store, ordering the product online and picking it up from a delivery point. It has a start and an end point: it runs from the realization of the need and ends with owning a product that satisfies the need.

- Consider this episode: "I have an issue." In the case of a broken electronic device, this episode may involve touchpoints, such as reading the user manual, reading the quick troubleshooting hints and FAQs on the product website, searching online forums for techy help, checking the warranty coverage, sending a "call back" request to the product helpdesk, diagnosing the technical issue with a support agent over the phone and having the broken device replaced at an authorized service point.

Episodes help to divide and design

We defined customer episodes as the distinct chapters of the customer journey. Considering that customer journeys are a wide-ranging and multi-faceted chain of events, customer episodes are useful divisions of the whole journey that can be designed and improved individually. However, we need to keep in mind that:

- Customer Journey cannot be fully divided into episodes that are mutually exclusive in terms of interactions (i.e. the same interaction may feature in two different episodes).

- Standalone optimization of customer satisfaction in each episode may not guarantee the highest level of overall satisfaction.

Guardianship of each episode may belong to different functions in the company. However, it is critical that one core cross-functional team works on the design of all episodes. Additional team members should be called in depending on the required expertise needed to design a specific episode.

Designing a customer journey is like preparing a complex meal

Think about it as a commercial kitchen in which the station chefs, cooks and kitchen assistants work in harmony to prepare a meal. Each station contributes to the final dish: the saucier station, the poissonnier/rôtisseur station, the entremetier station, the pâtissier station. At the end, the customer receives a beautiful plate and enjoys the enticing flavors. Designing a customer journey is no different than preparing a complex meal for the satisfaction of customers.

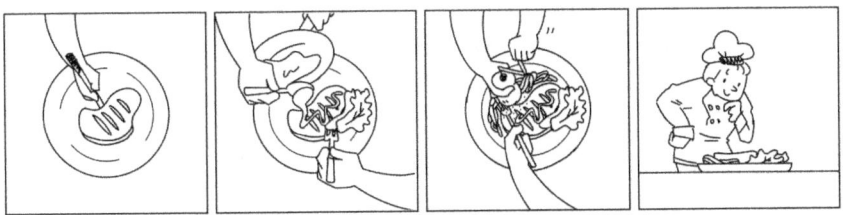

It is obvious that functional silos harm the customer experience more than anything else, from design to delivery. Traditionally, customer channels are controlled by different functional groups in companies, such as retail stores by Sales, contact centers by Customer Care, website and app by Marketing or Digital. None of the functions have an end-to-end view on how all planned activities come together and what the customer experiences in total. There is no doubt that every function is putting their best effort in place to maximize their contribution to the customer experience. However, without fully aligned processes, practices, incentives and management willpower, businesses risk performing worse than what the collective effort warrants. Developing distinguished experiences for your customers requires strong collaboration across the functions, which are used to operating independently: Product Development, Sales, Marketing, Customer Care, Digital, as well as your business partners in advertising and retail execution, should all be working closely together, if possible in the same physical and virtual "customer experience design" workspace, to craft the touchpoints and episodes.

CHAPTER 2

Human-Minded Care

Customer care is frequently associated with the image of a call center agent wearing headphones and smiling confidently. This is not a totally incorrect image as the call center is an important point of service delivery. However, it is far away from fully depicting what customer care is all about. Customer care stretches well beyond the boundaries of a call center. We will explore the fundamentals of customer care in detail throughout this book. However, as a first step, we will start by investigating what "care" really means as a standalone word.

Care is the provision of what is needed

Care is the provision of whatever is needed for the protection or well-being of a living thing or object. Not surprisingly, the first word that comes to my mind, when someone says care, is my mother. Motherhood is the epitome of care in nature. Mothers have a natural instinct to care for their children, showing strong affection and attention. Their care extends from the birth of their child to, in most cases, the end of their own lives. They expect nothing in return other than for their children to grow up to be good adults, to have a good education and occupation and, more than anything else, to love them back.

Motherhood as the epitome of care in nature

Building on the motherhood analogy, we can define customer care as providing whatever your customers need to benefit the most out of having your products in their lives. The positioning of the customer care function in a company should be similar to that of a mother in a family. It should be the heart of a company, which shows affection and attention to customers, without expecting anything directly in return (at least, at face value) - even if, deep inside, it is okay to expect your customers to love you back, to be loyal and to promote your products. A mother is the happiest when she hears her children say "my mother is the best in the world." A company should feel the most blessed when their customers make a similar claim: "you know, these guys are the best."

"Human-minded care" is about providing what is essential: physically to the human body, logically to the human mind and emotionally to the human soul

Human-minded care is an approach that encompasses the best practices of customer care. It is positioning "care for humans by humans" as an overarching principle that guides every activity you do. It is putting the quality of the human experience at the core of your business practice – in every point of interaction. It is about asking yourself the question, "Is this the best for my customers?" in every decision-making process. It is about defending the position, "Humans matter more than the rest," when the discussion is ruled by achieving short-term commercial objectives. Human-minded care does not mean bribing your customers with endless perks and gifts: mothers don't spoil their kids with countless presents either. It is about providing what is essential to the human body, mind and soul.

If love is the purpose, constancy is the secret

Human-minded care is the process of creating affection among your customers towards your brand based on the way you take care of them. It is about creating warmth. At the end of a long journey, accumulation of warmth (or coldness) determines whether your customers love you or hate you. Humans have certain mechanics informing the ability to love something and that is the result of a course of events: it does not happen all at once. You would not love someone just because he bought you a nice bouquet of flowers, took you out for a marvelous dinner, wrote you love poems or was there for you when you were sick. It is not one single act, but the consistent accumulation of many acts which creates the feeling of love.

Constancy to purpose is the secret formula for making someone love you. Humans love the ones who care for them. Humans also come to love products the same way. A group of researchers recently explored whether the consumer brand relationships and interpersonal relationships rest upon the same neurobiological underpinnings (Fürst, 2015). They tested the role of oxytocin (known as the "love hormone") in the formation of a bond between consumers and brands. They identified a substantial increase in endogenous oxytocin release following exposure of consumers to their favorite brand. Accordingly, they concluded that oxytocin plays a fundamental role in forming relationships with brands – similar to its role in developing interpersonal relationships.

We don't necessarily know when we began to love someone (or something), but we almost always know when we no longer love someone (or something). The most important thing to keep in mind is that customers are humans and care is an activity where humans take care of other humans. This is the starting point for human-minded care and building on trust to develop an emotional bond: transforming a brand first into one that is trusted, then into one that is loved. You don't need to engage in spontaneous emotional acts to develop an emotional bond: consistent flow of well-thought-out acts is the secret. You can even call it the art of charming, if you'd like.

Sympathy, empathy, compassion: it is all about building trust

Here, I am not referring to an endless flow of sympathy (understanding others) or empathy (feeling for others). These qualities are often praised in care; they are necessary, but not sufficient on their own. Think about not feeling well and paying a visit to a doctor (a medical care professional trained to take care of humans). What do you expect? Do you expect her to show genuine sorrow about your situation? Do you expect her to hold your hand and moan with you? Do you expect her to take the situation as if it were personal? Do you expect her to tell you about her own sickness or sicknesses in her family? Presumably, not!

What do you really expect? You expect the doctor to do her best to alleviate your suffering as a priority. You expect full presence, responsiveness and readiness. In short, you expect the sympathy and empathy to progressively turn into compassion and action.

One only truly trusts if one observes compassion: one needs to feel confident about being heard, being understood and being in capable hands. Have you ever felt disconnected (not physically, but mentally) from a service agent that you were talking with over the phone? Have you ever felt that his responses didn't resonate with your situation? Have your ever called back for the same issue with the hope to talk to another service agent? If you ever have done that, what was the missing ingredient? Trust? Without trust, every interaction is half-done. Sympathy, empathy and compassion are vehicles to facilitate building trust: they are means, but not the objective.

Big in Japan, but elsewhere?

The Japanese philosophies of *omoiyari* (anticipating customer needs before they are voiced) and *omotenashi* (selfless hospitality) are frequently mentioned in the context of superior care-taking. In Japan, you may observe those philosophies in the acts of airport workers realigning the luggage in the right direction on the conveyer belt, elevator operators dressed immaculately, taxi drivers with white gloves using handles to open your door from inside, hosts escorting you from the entrance of the restaurant to your table while carefully pointing out every step up and down on the way, and people bowing everywhere. You might even physically feel the warmth of care when you sit on a heated toilet seat.

These philosophies are embedded deep inside the Japanese culture: Japanese people are brought up with those values. Service, at the highest quality possible, is an integral part of the product (goods or services) in Japan: you don't pay extra for it. You don't tip to reward it. Tipping is seen as socially unacceptable. Trying to implement these philosophies in another culture is close to impossible: think about the other extreme, where a waitress feels comfortable throwing a hostile look at customers who only tipped her 12% after terrible service. On the flip side, anticipation of needs could be seen as superficial overprediction and subsequent violation of personal space in some cultures, especially in face-to-face interactions. We need to keep in mind that customer expectations and subsequent reactions elsewhere are not necessarily the same as in Japan. This style of humans taking care of other humans works in Japan because of shared cultural values regarding service: anticipation, enthusiasm, self-sacrifice and high-quality. You can surely be amazed and inspired by these philosophies. However, as these philosophies are cultural and dependent on human expectation and execution, they cannot possibly be replicated anywhere outside of Japan.

Consistency in excellence is the key differentiator of care

People will always be at the core of your care practice. Nevertheless, I think the challenge is to deliver on a set of values – like anticipation, enthusiasm and trustworthiness – without leaving it solely to the capabilities and willingness of individuals: your ability to eliminate personnel-based circumstantial variations, to the extent possible, will define and differentiate your care practice. We defined love as a product of consistent repetition of a warmth-creating behavior. Businesses can only achieve consistency in excellence by developing proper policies, processes and systems, and deploying them relentlessly. It all starts with making "care first" as one of your guiding principles and structuring a proper governance around this principle.

"Care-first" as a guiding principle

Nordstrom, the department store chain based in Seattle, US, is frequently cited as a leader in customer care. Nordstrom scores a long-term average [1995-2018] above 80 in the American Customer Satisfaction Index (ACSI) and ranks as the top performer in the Department & Discount Stores category, alongside Costco. There are many publicly recited stories about Nordstrom employees going above and beyond to help customers in stressful situations. I won't repeat these stories here. All these stories are a great read and can be quickly found online. Our focus is on how Nordstrom defines care as a guiding principle and creates a company culture that makes these stories come true.

Nordstrom's Code of Business Conduct and Ethics starts as follows:

"Our number one goal is to provide outstanding customer service. To support this, we have One Rule: Use Good Judgement. We expect you to use good judgment when it comes to taking care of our customers, each other and our vendors."

Our service promise since 1901.

The aspiration to deliver outstanding customer service is embodied in Nordstrom's service promise. It is the simplest service promise possible, just made of a three-letter word: "Yes." Nordstrom's care-first intention and customer satisfaction track record are undisputable. However, whether Nordstrom can say yes to every service request or whether all can be left to the good judgement of the employees is highly debatable. Actually, Nordstrom's "One Rule: Use Good Judgement" is a myth. The company has detailed rules on many topics, all available online, which leave room for no further interpretation. This is not surprising, as good judgement is an overly subjective criterion to consistently handle millions of customer cases. Therefore, the good judgement rule should be interpreted as an overarching one that drives all other rules and an inspirational guideline that drives the decision-making process when an unclear situation (not covered by any rules) is faced.

The care-first principle should drive the definition of policies with humans in mind, by humans for the benefit of other humans, in a way that would make you happy if you were the customer on the other side of the interaction. Nordstrom's famous return policy is the typical example.

Table 2. Nordstrom's return policy

"We handle returns on a case-by-case basis with the ultimate objective of making our customers happy. We stand behind our goods and services and want customers to be satisfied with them. We'll always do our best to take care of customers – our philosophy is to deal with them fairly and reasonably. We have long believed that when we treat our customers fairly, they in turn are fair with us."

This policy is the underlying driver of the legendary stories of Nordstrom accepting returns without receipts or product tags, even a year after purchase, and, in one extreme case, accepting the return of a product that Nordstrom's didn't sell in the first place. The expectation of mutual trust and fairness, between the business and the customers, is the signature of Nordstrom's policy.

Principles and policies are necessary, but not sufficient. Having well-defined processes in place and ensuring proper execution of these processes, through rigorous personnel training and deployment of enabling technologies, set the way to the consistency in excellence. This may all sound like striving for a rigid governance system, but it is not. Flexibility and progression should be two defining values to sufficiently balance any rigidity. Flexibility is especially needed in the face of new business initiatives and changing market conditions. Whenever and wherever required, flexibility should be achieved by the intervention of trained, motivated people to resolve the cases by applying your guiding principles. Each resolution should help us learn more and predict better, eventually developing new policies and processes. Customer insights and business indicators will also necessitate changes: our governance system should be like a living organism being fed by these calls. This feed is key to the progression that will keep the system relevant over time.

Care is the practice, Customer Care is the function

At this stage, it is important to clarify how we differentiate between care practice and care function. We define "customer care" or, simply "care" as the practice of delivering what is essential to the customers. Care is a responsibility of all business functions. "Customer Care," on the other hand, is the function that ensures the application of care principles and progress towards the achievement of care objectives. Therefore, care is the accountability of the Customer Care function.

The term customer service is frequently used as a synonym for customer care. We can define customer service as the assistance and advice provided by a company to those who buy or use its products. Service is an important element of care. However, care should stretch well beyond the service and become part of everything you do. Restricting your care practice to service only puts you in an inferior position from the get-go.

I would like to think service as a late act of care. In many cases, if the right care were practiced at earlier stages of customer relationship, no service would be needed. For instance, the customer wouldn't need to call the helpdesk if the promotion mechanics were effectively communicated to her in the first place. Or her device wouldn't be broken if she had been properly onboarded. As services play a fundamental role in the delivery of care objectives, especially by correcting what has not been done satisfactorily earlier in the process, the Customer Care function is best suited to be responsible for service delivery. We will discuss this topic more at length in upcoming chapters.

CHAPTER 3

The Changing Role of Customers & Customer Care

As cultural values shift, means of communication change, and technology advances, the role of the customer and customer care evolve as well. Considering the increasing importance of establishing a strong relationship with each and every single customer, customer care is poised to become more critical for businesses. Customer care will help some businesses pave their way to success and prosperity whereas the others, especially the ones that can't read and act on the change, will inevitably fail. Accordingly, it probably makes sense to devote a chapter to explore the evolution of customer and customer care.

The changing role of customers

What do customers do? They use your products and talk about them. Businesses operate to generate earnings by selling products to their customers: in that sense, we can refer to the Customer Lifetime Value (CLV) metric and define the value of a customer to a business as follows by using the traditional CLV formula:

Present value (PV) of the earnings during the expected period of the business relationship less the cost of acquisition ($C_{acquisition}$), where the earnings are defined as the revenue (R) minus the cost of products sold (COGS)

$$\text{CLV} = \Sigma_{t=1}^{T} PV \, [R_t - COGS_t] - C_{\text{acquisition}}$$

T: Expected duration of the relationship between the business and customer (usually expressed in years)

Loyalty is the lifetime purchase of your products

Loyalty is customer's devotion to your product, as measured by his current commitment to purchase and the likelihood to continue purchasing in the future. We can define the customer loyalty based on two parameters: the amount of revenue the customer generates for the business year on year basis (R_t) and the duration of relationship (T) – in other words, the number of years the revenues would continue.

However, this traditional formulation is inadequate in fully valuating the customer, as it ignores the "talking" element, i.e. word-of-mouth. As customers use your products, they form an opinion about them and start sharing these opinions with those around them. This collaboration was limited to those in close proximity before the invention and propagation of remote communication means. In parallel to increasing access to the internet and experience-sharing platforms, customers of the digital era are more empowered and collaborative than ever before. Thereby, opinion sharing has become a more critical customer function.

Customers do more than just buy your products:
they communicate

Modern interpretations of CLV include the economic value of the promoting (or demoting) role of customers to some extent: in modified formulas, the frequently made modification is to incorporate the present value of earnings from the customers acquired through referrals by earlier customers. This is a clear improvement over the traditional formula; nevertheless, even the modified formulation is far away from fully reflecting the word-of-mouth value of customers.

In terms of conceptualization, customers can best be defined as an earned or incentivized communication channel. As opposed to owned and controlled channels, customers may act in both directions: they may advocate or disparage through creating impressions. Happily using a product in the presence of others leaves a positive impression. It is a passive but genuine referral. Engaging in a dispute at a retail store in front of other potential and current customers gives another impression: presumably, one that doesn't work in your favor. Businesses strive for positive impressions, like the customer mentioning the product (randomly) in a conversation or posting a photo on social media which (unintentionally) features the product. The usual approach for businesses is to do their best in treating their customers while hoping that customers would notice their efforts. However, it is also common to see businesses trying tit-for-tat strategies, such as incentivizing their customers to generate positive impressions in exchange of some benefits.

Without getting lost in complex mathematical formulations, we can redefine the CLV and modify the above formula as follows:

> Present value of the earnings and impressions generated by a customer less the cost of acquiring and interacting with that customer

$$CLV = \Sigma_{t=1}^{T} PV\,[MC_t] + \Sigma_{t=1}^{T} (PV[I_t^+ - I_t^-] - PV\,[C_t^{ci}]) - C_{\text{acquisition,}}$$
$$where$$

> MC_t: marginal contribution (earnings; revenue minus the cost of products sold)
>
> I_t^+: value of positive impressions

I_t^-: value of negative impressions

C_t^{ci}: cost of direct customer investment (i.e. loyalty and retention programs, services, incentives)

We will not dive into the details of calculating the value of impressions. Understanding the formulation at a conceptual level is sufficient to facilitate the future discussions in this book. All businesses aim to maximize the CLV; or, at least, to have a positive CLV.

If we reorganize the formulation above, CLV is positive only if:

$$\Sigma_{t=1}^{T} PV [MC_t + I_t^+] > \Sigma_{t=1}^{T} PV [I_t^- + C_t^{ci}] + C_{acquisition}$$

We will refer to this formulation as the CLV balance equation in the rest of the book. As the Cost of Acquisition is a sunk cost for any existing customer, the CLV optimization exercise boils down to maximizing the difference between the present value of a customer's contribution through use of products and making positive impressions and the present value of the cost of direct customer investment (i.e. retention, service and incentives) and overcoming the damage caused by negative impressions. For potential customers, the Cost of Acquisition could be seen as an extra hurdle to overcome in the equation.

Advocacy is the difference between positive and negative impressions generated

We can define customer advocacy based on the difference between the value of positive and negative impressions generated by a customer. If the value of positive impressions exceeds the negative, the customer is a net promoter. Otherwise, he is a net detractor. It is important to highlight that the cost associated with one negative impression is usually more than the benefit associated with one positive impression in interactions of similar nature, as:

- Customers talk more about poor experiences than good ones. According to the Global Customer Service Barometer (American Express, 2017), customers tell two times more anecdotes about negative experiences than positive ones.

- People are more receptive to bad news than to good news. Poor experiences tend to result in a disproportionate amount of chatter and consequent damage to brand credibility.

It is also important to understand how direct customer investment affects loyalty and advocacy in the formulation above. Two loyalty parameters – expected period of business relation (T) and earnings (MC), as well as the balance of impressions – heavily depend on direct customer investment (C_t^{ci}) among other factors, such as product performance or competitive product offering. Having said that:

- The more monopolistic the industry is, the less is the impact of direct customer investment on the loyalty parameters due to the absence or shortage of competitive offers. Therefore, monopolistic businesses have limited motivation to invest in customers and deliver good care: obviously, this lack of investment increases the CLV and makes financial sense. As a general rule, we can assume that the more monopolistic the industry is, the worse the care. Just think about the horror stories about customers dealing with former state monopolies in the service industry: the image of people waiting in long lines, filing long forms to submit requests and never receiving a reply regarding when their requests might be fulfilled.

■ No one will continue to use a failing product just because the care taking is stunningly great. In highly competitive industries, in the sense that the core product differentiation is low (i.e. no product is failing versus the others), the importance of care amplifies: companies try to gain differentiation through care. It is the pathway to a positive brand connotation in consumers' mind though an image of excellence. On the flip side though, customers become more inclined to leave a brand if it fails to deliver on its care promise. All in all, direct customer investment becomes more critical.

In this book, we are focusing on competitive industries and, thereby, businesses that are motivated to invest in their customers. Another relevant interpretation of the CLV balance equation would be based on comparing a business cutting the corners in service to reduce costs with a business investing in delivering a superior experience:

■ The cost-cutting business would have to compensate the loss of goodwill caused by the low-quality service and, thereby, would suffer from a higher cost of negative impressions: one component in the Right-Hand Side (RHS) of the equation will go down whereas the other will go up. Will the business be better off? It depends on the relative magnitude of rebalancing.

■ In contrast, the investing business would suffer from higher service costs. However, it would benefit from the extended lifespan of the business/customer relationship and increased customer spending – as well as the additional positive impressions created by the customers who enjoy the improved service delivery. Direct customer investment causes both sides of the CLV balance equation to go up. Will the business be better off? It depends on how wisely the investment is made.

To sum it up, providing good care could increase customer loyalty (i.e. how often a customer buys from the company and the amount of money each customer spends on the company's products) and advocacy (i.e. "happy customers bring new customers" by spreading the good reputation). Next, we will take a look into loyalty and advocacy in the context of care in a bit more detail.

Loyalty

There is a common agreement among academics and practitioners that acquiring a new customer is more costly than retaining an existing one. Exactly how much more costly? There is no agreement on that: a wide range of numbers have been proposed. This is not surprising because the answer depends on the industry and the state of the industry in terms of maturity (i.e. its collective potential of generating new customers) and competitiveness. Depending on the industry analyzed, academics have come up with a range of multiples such as five to twenty-five times (Gallo, 2014).

The more loyal your business is to your customers, the more loyal your customers will be to your brand. Modern care is about being an advocate of customers inside the company, and the success in doing so is dependent on the commitment to put your customers' needs, wants, preferences and issues at the core of every activity. Customer loyalty, among other factors, is dependent on making it pleasant for the customers to interact with your business. Pleasant could mean intuitive, quick or without excessive effort. It could also mean better than the expectations established in the customers' minds (for example, expedited versus regular shipping). Every contact with your customers is an opportunity to improve your reputation in the marketplace and increase the likelihood of repeat sales. From the courtesy of the contact center personnel to the efficiency of your order-fulfilment systems, every aspect of your business affects the way the customers view you. Delivering a consistently pleasant experience is more relevant for loyalty than delivering stunning experiences once in a while, as customers have the tendency to punish painful experiences more eagerly than to reward the fantasies.

Sometimes, businesses see gifting as a shortcut to building loyalty. Improving customer happiness through gifting is not a sustainable practice. It is likely that you will make your customer happy the first time you offer them a gift. This unexpected gesture creates a positive surprise and produces brief happiness. You may have similar results the second time you offer a gift. However, over time, receiving a gift becomes an expectation. If you gift, you meet expectations but you are not necessarily making customers happy. If you don't gift, you fail to meet their expectations – presumably causing unhappiness. Customer happiness is like the stock market: the share prices don't move based on absolute business results. They move based on the business results relative to the market expectations. You make your customer happy as long as you meet or beat the inherent expectations. This does not mean that you should not gift your customers. You should. However, there should be a clear reason why you gift and the reason should be more relationship related, rather than compensation for a product or service failure. It is important to explain to the customer why you are offering a gift on that special occasion in order to minimize the risk of gifting becoming an expectation.

Gifts should be intentionally selected. Don't offer a meaningless gift just for the sake of offering it. For instance, a friend of mine recently received discount coupons from two health and beauty chains for her birthday. One chain was offered $5 discount on her next purchase. She was frustrated with this gift: she thought that receiving a $5 gift was an insult considering that she regularly spent hundreds of dollars in this chain. The other chain offered 10% discount on her next purchase of $50 or above. She was happy with this gift as she perceived a 10% discount to be of good value. Gifting a loyal customer on her birthday is a good practice to build loyalty. However, a poorly selected gift, as in the case of the first health and beauty chain, could make you lose a loyal customer rather than earning her loyalty. You should care and be careful even when you are gifting your customers.

Advocacy

Customers play an increasingly important role in spreading information. The basic objective for any business is to have their customers spread the positive word about their products to a greater number of potential customers. As mentioned before, there are two broad strategies that can be deployed to achieve this objective:

- **Organic word-of-mouth:** The product has news value. There is something unique or unusual to talk about: for instance, a new or better experience. This is active word-of-mouth. There is also passive word-of-mouth – we simply use the product and others see (or hear) us using and enjoying it. In either case, word-of-mouth is an organic process that you cannot control: you strive to do better than the others and hope that your efforts will be realized by the customer. Moreover, it works in both directions: there is both positive and negative word-of-mouth.

- **Induced word-of-mouth:** We are paid to talk about the product. If you are a celebrity or an influencer, you may even be paid to use the product. If your endorsement is not worthy of pay (as is the case for most of us), you may still enjoy direct or indirect monetary benefits by referring your friends, family members or other acquaintances.

According to the Global Trust in Advertising (Nielsen, 2015) report, based on proprietary online research polling 30,000 respondents from 60 counties, 83% of consumers trust recommendations from people they know. This research confirms that acquaintance recommendation is more trusted than any other form of advertising. Moreover, consumers still trust the views of other consumers even if they don't know the person. For instance, consumer opinions posted online come across as a highly trusted medium, gathering the trust of two-thirds of the respondents and scoring better than any form of paid advertising. This fact makes peer-to-peer referrals and word-of-mouth generation a major focus area for marketers. How do you turn your most loyal customers into your salesforce? That is a trendy topic with no easy answer. Marketers develop solutions to trigger more word-of-mouth and referrals. There is nothing wrong in attempting to develop a salesforce out of your customers, provided that it is done with care. For example: directly approaching customers and inviting them to be part of a customer advocacy program through a random phone call could be seen as pushy and disturbing. Moreover, not every customer necessarily has a promoting (extrovert) profile. Many customers may perceive such a cold call as a careless act. Customers are not stupid. You should not even try to outsmart your customers; they understand that they are being used. Should you really take the risk of losing an otherwise loyal customer? Ultimately, while trying to acquire new customers, you may end up losing your existing customers if your acts are careless.

The better approach would be first to identify the customers who truly enjoy using your products. For instance, you may approach the customers who score you well in surveys through a less intrusive channel, such as e-mail or direct message, and offer them a win-win scheme in case they would like to make referrals. Almost all direct-to-consumer startups are successful in implementing this strategy. Uber is one great example. They are able to track the frequency of use of their service and the ratings given after service use for each customer. They invite the customers who are confirmed to happily use their service to their referral program via e-mail. "Show your friends you care," reads the tagline of their typical invitation. Their win-win scheme is that the referred friend will save $10 on their first ride while the one who refers will also save $10 on the next ride. This is an example of a well-designed campaign, supported with the inherent data analysis and artificial intelligence capabilities of the platform.

Organic word-of-mouth should be the ultimate aspiration for any business. Delivering a new or better experience through care has news value and could trigger customer talk. However, this is a hard-won battle. Accordingly, serious effort is required to trigger a wave of positive word-of-mouth whereas even simple failures could trigger a wave of negative word-of-mouth. The first objective should be avoiding the negative. Recent events have more news value than the earlier ones: your earlier investments in creating customer delight could easily be washed out by one recent failure. Customer acquisition, through word-of-mouth, is a function of delighting the customer: giving them something to talk about. Wowing customers may lead to advocacy for a limited period of time; however, it doesn't guarantee sustained loyalty by any means.

Balancing loyalty and advocacy

It is unanimously agreed that acquiring a new customer is more costly than retaining an existing one. However, whether you have an aggressive (acquisition oriented) or defensive (retention oriented) strategy depends on your company's position in the industry. Obviously, no start-up would have a defensive strategy as start-ups don't have much to defend. It is all about retention for the distant leaders in stagnant/mature markets. In any case, the most practical way to interpret the above statement is: ensure retention before acquisition and make sure that acquisition does not come at the expense of retention. In customer care terms, don't try to wow your customers (for the sake of word-of-mouth generation) before ensuring the delivery of a consistently high level of care.

Ensure retention before attempting acquisition

Here is a practical example. Think about a customer who sees a campaign online and upgrades his internet subscription to the more expensive, ultra-high-speed option. He orders the new subscription online. He is excited about enjoying the fast download speed and uninterrupted streaming with his new subscription package. However, that experience is still 48-72 hours away as his modem is old and he needs to receive and install a newer one for the ultra-high-speed connectivity. The modem will arrive to his address by post. Later that day, he receives an e-mail from his internet provider, thanking him for the purchase and, more importantly, informing him that they will send him the new modem by special courier. As a result, he will receive his new modem by the end of the business day. What a great surprise! Just around 5:00 PM, he receives his new modem in a nicely wrapped package. And, that is not all! He also receives a code which allows him to watch a paid movie of his choice for free as a small gift of appreciation for his continued trust in his internet provider. Another great surprise! This is an example of great cross-selling for the internet provider, which also sells TV subscriptions. One stone, two birds: both reward the loyal customer and have him try paid streamlining service just at the right moment (right as he gets his ultra-high-speed connection). A great finale for the story would be the customer tweeting about their service excellence and starting to spread that positive word-of-mouth.

Turning back to our customer, he is even more excited about the new subscription than before. He immediately calls his girlfriend to meet for a movie night. Now he needs to install the new modem, order pizza and open a bottle of red wine. He takes out the modem and the installation manual. It seems a bit more complicated than what he expected, but no problem: he is tech-savvy. He connects all the cables, but the modem is not responding. He needs help. Normally, he would google it, but he does not have much time before his girlfriend arrives, so he calls the helpdesk. He presses three for technical support and starts waiting. He waits, waits, waits. While waiting, he listens to some irritating on-hold music, which is interrupted occasionally with a more irritating voice saying, "your call is important to us, thank you for waiting." Thirty minutes pass and no one answers his call as all agents are busy with other customers (most likely, the campaign is working well and the internet provider is receiving tons of requests from new subscribers or upgraders). After waiting for an hour and thirty minutes, after his pizza and girlfriend arrive, he hangs up and swears from the bottom of his heart. He will still enjoy his rewarmed pizza with his girlfriend, but there is one more thing to do quickly beforehand: he will tweet about this ridiculous internet provider of his. He is a techy guy – his friends take his opinion seriously.

I am pretty sure you all have had similar experiences in your life as a customer and you understand the essence of the story. What went wrong in this story for the internet provider? They invested in wowing the customer by delivering the new modem with a speedy courier service and offering a paid movie for free. Yet they failed in the basics. During the campaign period, when sales and subsequent support requests are expected to sky-rocket, they failed to plan extra capacity at their contact center. While pushing for extra word-of-mouth, they risked retaining a loyal and highly profitable customer. In the end, they ended up with an unsatisfied customer.

Customer Satisfaction is the difference between the perceived performance and expectations

Customer Satisfaction is a measure of how well a customer's need is fulfilled, as defined by the difference between the performance perceived by the customer and her built-in expectations. At every touchpoint, we should aim to meet and exceed the customer's expectations. However, what matters the most is how the customer feels at the end of an episode – that is to say, when her need is addressed (or has failed to be addressed) rather than how she feels after a touchpoint. For instance, delivering a high level of customer satisfaction at every touchpoint does not warrant a high level of overall satisfaction if the customer needs to go through an excessive number of touchpoints. In that sense, the fewer the touchpoints needed to address a customer need, the higher the customer satisfaction. As an episode is a chain of events, touchpoints and channels cannot be optimized in a standalone manner.

Overall satisfaction builds up (or down) throughout the episode

Overall satisfaction in an episode could be defined as the multiplication of the customer satisfaction (CSAT) achieved at every touchpoint less the residual dissatisfaction resulting from the extra effort caused by the imperfect integration of different touchpoints and channels.

Overall satisfaction = $\prod_{i=1}^{n} CSAT_i$ – Residual Dissatisfaction

i: touchpoints in an episode (n, in total)

Let's clarify the theory with a practical example. I once bought a mobile phone from a niche manufacturer. The phone was ultra-small compared to the well-known models on the market: I was able to fit it in the coin pocket of my jeans. I am still not sure about the personal customer need that led to this purchase – it was a rather impulsive purchase and I was intrigued by the unique design and size. However, my excitement did not last long as I was not able to recharge the phone. As an immediate reaction, I read the user manual and FAQs on the website, and searched online user forums. That's already three touchpoints since the start of the episode. Not being able to quickly fix the issue, I went back to where I bought the device (a multi-brand store). They tried a few things, like pressing multiple buttons or recharging with different chargers, but none of them worked. They advised me to directly contact the manufacturer. They also gave me a nice piece of (branded) fabric to clean the screen of the smartphone. At the fourth touchpoint, my issue was still not addressed, but I was not unhappy either. I pressed the half smiley face (rating 4 on a 5-scale satisfaction survey) while leaving the store.

The manufacturer only offered an e-mail contact option with no possibility to give them a call. This was not surprising for a niche manufacturer with a limited service infrastructure. I wrote them an e-mail. They replied back kindly and promptly: they asked for my phone number as we needed to do some troubleshooting over the phone. I subsequently received their satisfaction survey and rated them as an 8 on an unusual 10-scale (rather than the typical 5-scale measure). Now, at the fifth touchpoint, I felt that I was on the right track. The troubleshooting call arrived later: I had to explain what I had written in the e-mail all over again. But, fine; she asked me to send the phone to their support center and gave me the address. She confirmed that they would be covering all the costs and, as a small compensation for my troubles, she would me sending me a specially designed leather phone pouch. I subsequently received their satisfaction survey and rated them as an 8 on the same unusual 10-scale. That was the sixth touchpoint: I was almost there.

At this point, I am skipping the complications caused by cross-border logistics for the sake of cutting the story short. Eventually, I sent the phone and, a few days later, I received a call from them: they told me that they would be replacing my old phone (never used) with a new one and I would be receiving it shortly. At the seventh touchpoint, the issue was finally resolved. I received the new phone and the leather pouch by post and another satisfaction survey by e-mail. I again rated them as an 8. Now, based on all the interactions and my four separate ratings, you may assume that I was 80% satisfied in this episode. I was not. Actually, my overall satisfaction was much lower than that.

The catch is that throughout the episode, the manufacturer bought my happiness – for a limited period of time – by offering me small gifts combined with the kindness of their service personnel. However, ultimately, I was dissatisfied. More concretely, at the end of this episode, I promised myself never again to buy a novelty gadget instead of a well-known product. I would rate my overall satisfaction from this episode one out of five, or 20%.

As previously discussed, the overall satisfaction from an episode is the multiplication of the satisfaction achieved at every touchpoint less the dissatisfaction resulting from the extra effort caused by the imperfect integration of different touchpoints and channels such as (1) the weakness of their self-help options (first three touchpoints), (2) the inability to contact them by phone, (3) the lack of integration between e-mail and phone channels and (4) the hassle of posting the old phone. If we do the math by revising the aforementioned formula:

$$20\% = (80\%)^4 - \text{Residual Dissatisfaction}$$

$$\text{Residual Dissatisfaction} \approx 20\%$$

We can conclude that the extra effort caused by the friction points (i.e. poor touchpoint and channel integration) resulted in 20% incremental dissatisfaction in this specific episode.

As a niche manufacturer whose new customer acquisition is heavily dependent on word-of-mouth, what could they have done better? Obviously, they could have avoided the issue in the first place by not selling a faulty device. Focusing excessively on the functionality and device aesthetics at the expense of device robustness (in the sense of occurrence of software and hardware defects) is a commonly observed pitfall for emerging niche players. In any case, defects do occur: but more frequently for some companies than the others. Knowing the type of frequently occurring defects is crucial. It is likely that battery failure was a common defect for that model: it could be that it was the result of a manufacturing batch issue, a material issue or a design weak point. The other critical point is the ease of service access. At the very least, voice service should be available in English – and maybe in a few other major languages – because diagnosing a technical failure using exclusively written communication takes a lot of effort. They could have placed their helpline number on the front page of the user manual and on the device packaging: "Need help? Call us at..." Knowing that they are weak in the self-help and face-to-face service channels, they could have channeled the service needs to the helpline. They could have immediately completed the fault-tree analysis over the phone and concluded that my device needed to be swapped with a new one. If the issue were a common issue with clear symptoms, they would not face a high no-fault-found risk (i.e. unnecessarily swapping a functional device). Instead of asking me to send my device back to them, they could have offered a two-way courier service: a courier to bring me the new device and pick up the old one. Accordingly, the episode could have been simplified into this: my device is not recharging, so I call them and find that my device needs to be replaced. I receive my new device by courier within a few days and hand over my old device. I receive the satisfaction survey soon after receiving the new device and rate them at 8 on the same 10-scale. This might be a more costly method of resolution for the manufacturer, but the result is that they retain my business and my positive word-of-mouth – which is what matters the most for a niche manufacturer.

The bottom line is that an episode fully carried out in one channel rather than in multiple channels is likely to result in higher customer satisfaction if interacting in multiple channels does not bring additional value or lower the effort for customers. After all, what is more important? Choice or excellence? Many half-baked solutions or one solid solution?

The overall satisfaction is an average

The overall satisfaction from the journey is the average of satisfaction achieved in each episode rather than a multiplication. Think about it like a sports league with a series of games. Each game is an episode with a clear start and finish: it is a continuous process. Each succeeding action builds on the previous ones and the result of a game depends on the outcome of all the actions taken during the game. You multiply your performance up or down as the game progresses. However, once the game is over, the next one starts from scratch. The season is a journey: it is a collection of discrete events. The success of a season depends on the average number of points collected in each game. For instance, you may have a disastrous performance in one game (i.e. handling a customer complaint): everything goes wrong and you lose heavily (i.e. 20% satisfaction). But in all other games, you may put forward a great performance and win convincingly (i.e. 80-100% satisfaction). Such a track record will result in a good overall performance – definitely not zero satisfaction, as if the multiplication were used instead of averaging out. The overall satisfaction from the journey is calculated based on a scorecard: if some episodes are proven to be more critical in terms of their contribution to the overall customer experience, you may even think about a balanced scorecard (with episodes having different weights in scoring).

Having said that one extremely poor performance may trigger an abrupt end of the relationship. Think about this case: if things get too ugly and your team engages in a fierce fist fight with the opponents after losing a game, it is likely that your players will be banned from playing or you will get expelled from the league for the rest of the season. Similarly, averaging out the satisfaction achieved in each customer episode is a valid approach as long as no individual performance is poor enough to cause a kneejerk reaction, i.e. a customer quitting your brand in frustration.

The changing role of the Customer Care function

Customer Care is traditionally perceived as a cost center and the executive focus has usually been on reducing the service costs (cutting the corners) without deteriorating customer satisfaction to a level that hurts. Customer Care is frequently regarded as operational or executional, rather than strategic: in some extreme cases, it is tossed under the marketing operations umbrella and has no clear identity. However, one simple fact has become more visible over the past decade or so: the Customer Care function interacts with customers on a broader range of occasions than any other function and generates more customer data-points than any other function. Smart executives are increasingly realizing that care should be at the core of customer experience design and delivery.

Care at the core of customer experience design and delivery

Customer Care is indeed responsible for a large piece of the customer journey. It directly interacts with thousands of customers, hearing the "voice of the customer" on a daily basis. Assuming the right processes and systems are in place, it has the ability to instantly take the pulse of the customer, while monitoring the overarching customer sentiment, pain points and emerging trends. Consequently, improvement opportunities for the company's overall offer, which could turn into differentiating factors and create competitive advantage, constantly present themselves to the Customer Care personnel. Nevertheless, functions such as Sales and Marketing are mistakenly assumed to have a better view and understanding of the customer, even in companies with no direct-to-customer sales and marketing practice. Smart executives are realizing that it is time to break the false assumptions and give Customer Care its seat at the table (or, even better, give them the lead for certain episodes) in defining the critical experience blocks and the customer journey. For instance, care insights could contribute to the elimination of any unusual rupture in the flow of events that causes customer pain points. In many companies, you may even observe that Customer Care faces difficulties in, for example, plugging in a seasonal tip on the website and app, because it must first go through the Marketing or Digital function. This rings true even if it is obvious that a customer-relevant tip could proactively eliminate thousands of inquiries. Removal of such a pain point from the customer journey would not only improve overall customer satisfaction but also help reduce the care costs by eliminating some low-value support activities.

Customer Care should collaborate with other commercial functions to design the desired customer experiences and achieve a unified view of the customer. Functional silos result in data silos. Only through an omnichannel approach, companies can construct a 360-degree, detailed view of each customer and the complete history of each interaction. A unified customer view facilitates the understanding of customer actions, needs, pain points, segmentation of customers, development of specific offers and improvement of services. This will eventually lead to improved loyalty and advocacy.

Customer Care, as a function, is a stakeholder in every customer episode and should be a core member of the cross-functional design team. Specifically, there are six episodes which should be safeguarded by the Customer Care function:

- I want to know about the product

- I want to sign up

- I want/need more information

- I have an issue

- I have a suggestion

- I am frustrated

These six episodes will be covered in detail in the following chapters.

Through its rebranded positioning, Customer Care is transforming from an operational cost center into a strategic, customer value generator. Its reactive approach of handling customers' questions and complaints whenever they present themselves, will be increasingly replaced by a proactive approach: being the customer companion and advocate while developing a mutual trust-based relationship with the customers. This type of engagement impacts the revenue side of the income statement and the bottom-line of the company while redefining care as a growth engine.

Customer Care as an internal sounding board

I believe Customer Care's modern role entails safeguarding the promises made to the customers. Do we promise only what we are able to deliver? How do we ensure the delivery of our promises? Do we deliver without any exceptions? What do we do if and when we fail to deliver? Here, I am not talking about brand promises such as "The World's Most Refreshing Beer," "The Ultimate Driving Machine" or "To inspire moments of optimism and uplift." These are usually vague and highly debatable statements. I am referring to the concrete statements that should be ensured through reliable internal processes. The most typical example is "lowest price available on the market." If this is the promise made to the customer, it is the Customer Care team's responsibility to have at its disposal a documented process that guarantees the lowest prices on the market. In collaboration with the campaign development, Customer Care should develop a compensatory scheme in case the lowest price is not achieved in a given case. Before your customers have to do it, your Customer Care team should act on the customers' behalf and challenge your practices: Customer Care, as an internal sounding board, will make your promises more bulletproof and your credibility among customers will increase over time as you consistently deliver on your promises. At the final analysis, it is better to fail in front of an internal customer than to fail in front of an actual customer.

Customer Care as a generator of customer insights

Before concluding this chapter, it is crucial to visit the increasing role of Customer Care in developing customer insights. Recording and analyzing the data generated by care interactions could lead to faster and cheaper knowledge generation than traditional market research cycles, while reducing the need to consult to the customers for research.

Customers receive way too many surveys. I remember my friend's comment after seeing the emoji-based, push-a-button survey in the airport toilet: "nowadays, you cannot even urinate without filling out a survey." Customers are tired of surveys. This survey fatigue alone is a cause of dissatisfaction as customers increasingly feel spammed by the number of surveys they receive. It is important to keep mind that asking for a customer's feedback has an implicit cost. You should ask for customers' feedback only if the potential benefits (to be achieved by making improvements based on the customer feedback) exceed the explicit (collection & analysis) and implicit (customer fatigue) costs. In other words, ask for feedback only if what you expect to learn will turn into actionable insights for improving customer retention and advocacy.

Many times, you don't need to ask customers; you just need to listen to them. Customer Care is often described as the "voice of the brand." But it should also be thought of as the "ear of the brand." The ability to create meaningful customer experiences hinges on the ability to listen to and truly understand customers. In every interaction, customers share their complaints, compliments, comments and ideas with you. They send you valuable feedback. If you interpret these signals correctly and manage to categorize them into a few recurring themes, they will guide you to what needs to be improved in the customer journey. There is no customer feedback more meaningful than customer inquiries. What you hear in a service point is not a hunch. It is experiential; it is behavioral. Think about exposing customers to your new product in a pre-market launch focus group. When asked, customers will make comments on what they like or dislike about the features, functionality and design of your product. However, their comments will be rather hypothetical considering that they don't actually use the product. Due to limited exposure to the product, they won't necessarily be able to imagine all the use cases (specific situations) that can be faced in real life. Then think about a different scenario. Think about a customer calling your contact center for an issue that she has experienced with the same product. Think about thousands of other customers calling for the same reason. That very specific issue is your unquestionable reality.

For many businesses, care-related activities generate the greatest amount of interactions with the customer and allow the accumulation of extensive information about each individual customer. Moreover, multiplied by millions, these interactions offer a rich source of knowledge provided that they are recorded and analyzed in a rigorous manner. However, service cases are usually classified and recorded by subject codes. Depending on the case and service agent's will, additional information may be recorded verbatim. All details are not necessarily captured and whatever is captured will depend on the agent's hunch. Such a structure does not allow a complete analysis and reveal in-depth insights. The real insights would be revealed and emerging trends would be spotted in a timely manner only with full analysis of the interaction. Technologies are emerging to record the full interaction and transpose the speech to text for big data analysis. We will have an extended discussion on these technologies in a subsequent chapter.

We can broadly categorize the information to be collected in this manner in two nonexclusive categories.

(1) Personal information that would allow you to craft specific solutions for that very customer: a well-designed interaction (a more relevant experience) will not only address customers' functional needs but also their need to feel special and important. Loyalty is strongly associated with the ability to attach emotional connections and to continuously reassure the customer about why your brand is the right choice.

(2) Collective information that would offer you an unbiased (behavior based, rather than claim based) and in-depth customer understanding: this understanding would allow you to drive forward the product and communication design in a way that improves your offer for all customers (or for a group of customers with similar needs and desires). For instance, what is the area that requires immediate intervention in your business? How to identify the first thing to improve/fix in a business is a question that occupies executives' minds every day. The answer is whatever causes the most pain to your customers. Trending topics in your customer requests will provide you with that information: a request will trend up only if there is an underlying failure that touches a significant number of customers. A request will trend down or disappear when the underlying failure is rectified.

Customer inquiries should drive continuous improvement efforts

Here is a practical example: you have just launched a promotion campaign, triggering a massive influx of inbound contacts on the promotion mechanics. Firstly, this could be an early indicator of the promotion's potential as customers seem to be interested. As a result, they contact your company in masses to learn more about it. This is good news. However, it also seems that your accompanying communication is not very clear as customers don't understand who is eligible for the promotion and how to subscribe to it. This is calling for an immediate intervention on the promotion communication, specifically regarding these two pieces of information. We should not forget that for each customer contacting you, there is a bunch of others with the same concern in mind but who don't care to reach out. Many eligible customers (i.e. your target audience, for whom you have designed the promotion campaign) may not participate because either they do not know whether they are able or they do not understand how to do so, limiting the overall impact of the campaign and presenting a huge lost opportunity for your business. You revisit your communications and subsequently eligibility and enrollment-related inbound contacts start to disappear from the trending topics lists. This means that the intervention has been successful. However, now a new topic seems to be trending up: how to use certain promotional benefits. This is frequently the case as the "use" questions follow the "subscribe" questions in the customer journey: once the earlier issue is addressed, the latter issue comes under the spotlight. Another intervention is called for: why not send out an e-mail to all the customers who have enrolled in the promotion campaign and inform (or remind) them about the mechanics of the promotion – specifically highlighting the elements that trigger the most confusion.

One interesting observation is that customers don't only tell you what to focus on; they also do the prioritization for you through their inquiries. For instance, in the example above, they tell you to focus on your eligibility and enrollment communication first and "how to use" communication thereafter. In this manner, your customers are in the driver's seat for your continuous improvement efforts.

Considering that we are living in a data-driven business environment, the insights collected by the Customer Care function become an intrinsic source of information that drive the business forward and shape the decision-making process both at the tactical and strategic level.

Our approach differs from the common practice

For the time being, we will wrap up this chapter by highlighting the six major differences outlined in this book vis-à-vis the customer care practices commonly observed in the industry. They are:

1. Care should be a defining element in any company's culture

There is nothing romantic or idealistic about this statement: it is purely commercial. A company is only as valuable as its customers. Actually, every company theoretically is owned by its customers. We can explain this concept by bending the financial definitions a bit. In finance, an owner's share of a company's assets is defined by the term "equity." It is the sum of paid-in capital (initial investment made by the company owners) and retained earnings – which is equivalent to the sum of all net income incurred in case of no dividend payouts:

Equity = Paid-in Capital (contributed by the investors) + Retained Earnings (contributed by the customers)

As the customers are the source of earnings, they are equity providers in any company – even if they have no ownership or dividend rights. Thereby, any business, at least on a theoretical level, can be defined as a partnership between the investors and customers.

The thinking behind this is more important than the definition itself. Customers are a source of equity and you had better look after them by making care a core element of everything you do in your business. No business can survive or grow otherwise. Customers own companies: companies do not own customers. Zappos, an online shoe and clothing retailer based in Las Vegas, US, is frequently referred to as the hallmark of service excellence. Zappos defines itself as a "service company that just happens to sell things" and its purpose as "to live and deliver WOW through service." They have a beautiful motto: "Zappos. Powered by Service." If we trust the accuracy of the publicly shared customer feedback, they seem to live up to the expectations created by this motto. However, we should take this motto to the next level in order to better represent the concept: "All companies are powered by Care."

2. Caring is not a sporadic and one-off exercise

The traditional approach to care is non-continuous: an interaction at a point in time. Our approach is continuous: multiple interactions throughout the customer journey. Leading companies show care in everything they do. Do you have a caring product design? Do you have caring packaging and features? Do you have caring communications? If you care in the first place, you don't need to service your customers later. Service, in a reactive style, is a mere firefighting activity.

3. An experiential approach should replace an issue-handling approach whenever and wherever possible

The traditional approach to care is reactive, departmental (silo-based), problem solving and service-delivery oriented, and requires execution based on strict operational metrics. Our approach is proactive, cross-functional, customer-experience oriented (i.e. assessed by its contribution to the overall experience, rather than a standalone metric like Customer Satisfaction or Customer Effort Score) and requires execution based on the collective quality of all interactions. It focuses on improving the customer experience by eliminating the underlying causes of frequent issues.

4. Care should be practiced in every customer channel, not only through contact centers

You cannot assign the responsibility of care to only certain channels. Care is an omnipresent activity: the silhouette of your care practice should be felt wherever the customer is and even if you are not there.

5. Care is not made up of execution only: it is a strategic area

Care plays an important role in the overall customer experience. Therefore, as the custodian of care, the Customer Care function should be involved in every stage of the customer journey design. Moreover, it should take the ownership in the fulfillment of certain customer needs. Buy-in of all functions, especially from those which traditionally and mistakenly position themselves as the "owner" of customers, is critical for the successful inclusion of Customer Care in the strategic decision-making process.

6. Customer Care should take the lead in reconciliation with unhappy customers

An unhappy customer causes more harm to your business than the contribution made by a happy customer. Therefore, reconciling with unhappy customers is more business-critical than making more customers happy. Customer Care should take ownership of this reconciliation process as:

- reconciliation requires us to understand the different ways in which we make customers unhappy and to develop remedies addressing the underlying causes of unhappiness. Thereby, the employees who hear the most frequently and extensively from customers are best positioned for the role.

- the employees who can position themselves as impartial mediators between the customers and the business are more likely to be successful in reconciliation. An overly motivated spokesperson (militant) of an interest cannot fit that role. For instance, by definition, the main role of Sales and Marketing is to promote your products: the conflict of interest is too profound and too visible to develop an impartial mediator out of these functions.

Up to now, we have seen that care, when defined and executed correctly, has so much more to offer than merely solving problems for the customer. Care has the capacity to reach far beyond the traditional call-center, error remediation model of the past. Rather than being a one-off, reflexive practice, care offers a business the opportunity to engage with its customers in a continuous and meaningful way which benefits the business and the customers alike. Rather than considering care as a means of rectifying a wrong, businesses that embrace care as a company-wide core competency open the door to long-term relationships with engaged customers, who are likely to offer loyalty, advocacy, constructive feedback, and a sense of belonging to the business. In other words, a care-first business, one that views care with indifference, will condition an indifferent customer from the moment of first contact onward. A business that views the well-being of its customer as paramount, however, will find itself promoted by a customer who cares back. Without wanting to sound cynical, it is worth noting that being a care-first business is ultimately the best thing you can do to take care of your business.

CHAPTER 4

Care in Everything We Do

Customer care is about how well you take care of your customers in everything you do, displaying genuine kindness and concern for your customers in every interaction. It is about consistently attaching importance to their needs and wants, across the board, and making them feel like they are being looked after. This definition goes well beyond the classical, narrow scope of service, which consists of informing customers about the available products, helping them purchase the product, helping them make use of the product and troubleshooting.

The modern definition of care focuses on two pillars: (1) understanding the needs of an individual customer and helping him find the right solution, (2) building an emotional connection based on mutual trust. The services listed above still make up an important part of the care exercise. An extended discussion of these services, revisited with a proactive approach (rather than the classical, reactive approach), will be presented in the following chapter in the form of six customer episodes. However, before embarking a discussion on services, this chapter focuses on how to introduce the genetic code of your care practice (guiding principles) into every aspect of your business, from the product design to the packaging to brand communication.

Foresight to act before the moment of truth

Coding your business with care genes becomes even more critical if your business has a limited service scope or possibility of direct interaction with the end user. Let's go back to the Nestlé and Mövenpick ice-cream example. It is obvious that Nestlé can't possibly know each and every ice-cream consumer in the same way that an ice-cream shop owner in a local neighborhood can. There are obvious additional benefits that the local ice-cream shop can offer the customer vis-à-vis Nestlé. One of these benefits is the full flexibility of ice cream flavor selection: for example, a pistachio, cherry and caramel combination which would probably be the selection of only a few people. On this front, Nestlé won't be able to compete. However, there should be opportunities to do better with regard to service and customization at mass scale. Actually, having a limited amount of direct interaction with the end consumers renders care principles more important.

Let's think about it. What does a consumer need most when eating ice-cream on a hot, summer day? Presumably, a napkin to wipe away the melting ice-cream. Why not include a small paper towel (or, preferably, a wet towel) in the ice-cream packaging? One could even roll the towel around the cone.

Here's another example: a friend of mine ordered high-heeled shoes online. She received the shoes and tried them on, but she still couldn't decide whether to keep them or send them back. At that moment, she realized that they had included a small transparent sachet in the box with a set of spare heel guards. She frequently complained about losing those heel guards as they got stuck in cracks while walking. This was an excellent example of foresight and proactivity in care. That was the tipping point: she decided to keep the shoes.

Corona, a global beer brand, set another great example. In 2019, Corona unveiled stackable cans that could be twisted to interlock them together. It is an innovative solution to reduce single-use plastic waste by eliminating six-pack rings. Corona noted that the system is strong enough to hold ten cans together. Using a state-of-the-art design, here Corona foresees and addresses the concerns of the consumer highly sensitive to environmental issues. Moreover, Corona makes it easier to carry the beer cans in the absence of a bag or tray. Ask yourself: before heading to the refrigerator or grocery store, how many times might you ask your friends whether they want a beer and find that five or six of them want one? How difficult is it to carry that many cans of ice-cold beer? Would it be easier if they were stackable?

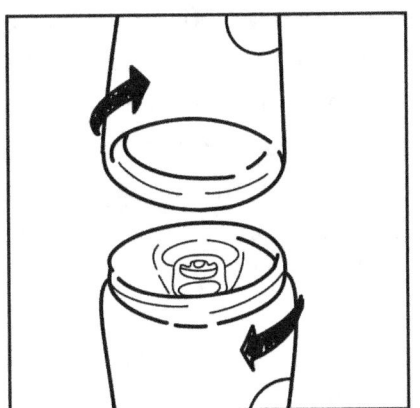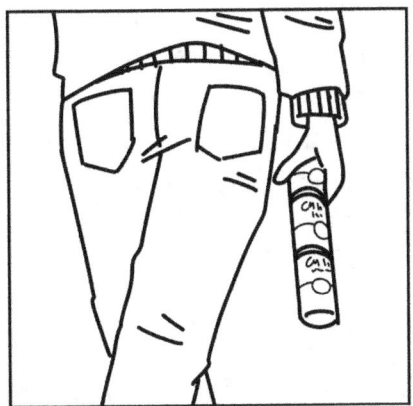

One final example is by Caffè Lattesso, a Swiss-based latte brand. How much consumer-relevant innovation can you really introduce into a takeaway latte product? A lot, if you really understand the consumer needs and wants. Two innovations really set Caffè Lattesso apart. One is the packaging design that includes a protective foil which keeps the lid hygienic and can easily be removed with one hand. This eliminates the risk of pulling too hard and spilling coffee all over. The other feature is that every Caffè Lattesso lid contains a small biscuit to be enjoyed with the coffee. This small surprise can bring the takeaway coffee experience to another level for many consumers.

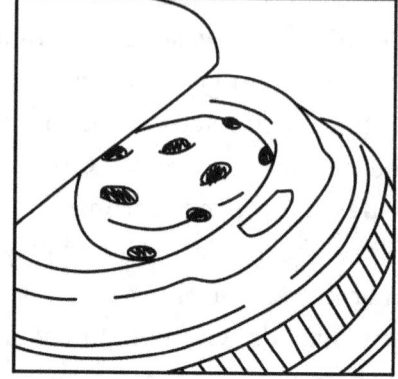

As highlighted in the examples above, in the case of limited direct interaction with the end-user, foresight regarding consumer needs and wants becomes even more critical. Businesses need to take action before the customer realizes that there is a need and faces an issue (i.e. placing a tissue in the ice-cream packaging, recognizing that the consumer might need one). Don't forget: good companies care even before the need for care is there.

Guiding principles of modern care

Making a difference through care hinges on our motivation and ability to design and execute everything we do as a business in a caring manner. Care is not a one-off activity or the sole responsibility of a few people in a business: it should be an enduring attitude for the whole business. Customers form a mental image of your brand based on the impression they develop interacting with your brand. As people face an extensive amount of information influx every day and have limited time (cognitive resource) and availability to process this information overload, they are obliged to take shortcuts. They form mental images based on a few (especially early) interactions. Customer Care's modern role involves making care part of this mental image from the start. It is about making customers feel that your business has genuine concern for their wants and needs, beginning with the very first interaction.

The caring attitude can be defined in seven guiding principles:

1. Be Simple: *The less complex, the better*

2. Be Passionate: *Care is a passion, not a fashion*

3. Be Honest: *Honesty is not optional*

4. Be Relevant: *Valuable only if relevant*

5. Be Long-lasting: *In it for the long haul*

6. Be Omnipresent: *Always there for you*

7. Be Consistent: *We are what we repeatedly do*

In the rest of this chapter, we will review these principles in detail.

(1) *The less complex, the better*

Do you care to make it simple for your customers? You should care because simplicity pays back. Siegel+Gale, a leading brand strategy and design firm, puts some figures behind the theory: according to their proprietary Global Brand Simplicity Index research (Siegel+Gale, 2018), 55% of consumers are willing to pay more for simpler experiences (loyalty) and 64% of consumers are more likely to recommend a brand because it provides simpler experiences and communication (advocacy).

We are all living under a nonstop shower of information. Businesses are racing with each other to deliver more through technology and innovation; information is produced and consumed quickly. The amount of information passing through our minds is growing at an exponential rate and we are overwhelmed by information processing. We are looking for simplification: simplicity is like a refreshing oasis to our brains. Simplicity reduces cognitive overload and builds trust. Complexity creates question marks, whereas simplicity offers solutions and answers. It induces the idea of "they thought about it a lot, they engineered it well, so I don't need to think about it." It eliminates the barriers to purchase, usage and recommendation. Actually, the more complicated the problem and the simpler the solution, the more the customer delight (positive experience). Maintaining simplicity and usefulness against increasing complexity is a key success factor. If one doesn't know what to do, then the best strategy is to do nothing: confused customers do nothing and they buy nothing.

In that sense, simple sells better. I was on a touristic Italian island a few years back. It was the perfect occasion for an authentic seafood experience. While scanning through the seafood restaurants in town, one of them caught my attention thanks to its tagline: "Solo pesce. Solo fresco. Solo la sera." That is to say, "Only fish. Only fresh. Only in the evenings." It was a restaurant with no menu – fixed price for all you can eat. They served what was caught and cooked that day and kept going for as long as I wished to continue eating: various hot and cold starters, shellfish, pasta and rice dishes with seafood and grilled fish, and Italian desserts. All were served directly from a large plate or bowl by waiters going around to the tables, and all were delicious. It was as simple as it gets, but it also provided all one might desire from an Italian restaurant, and all at a fixed price. Compare this with other restaurants on the island, offering a wide choice of starters, first courses, second courses and desserts. These many options and nuances between dishes might be important for locals, but might also prove to be overwhelming for a tourist looking for a memorable seafood night while on vacation. The restaurant I chose offered customers what they wanted and nothing more: it hit the bull's eye.

Simplicity is synonymous to customer-centricity

Simplicity is synonymous to customer-centricity. What does it take to get there? Above all, it takes time and effort to know your customers well enough to understand what they need in terms of product information, functionality and features. Simplicity requires working backwards, starting from what customers need. However, knowing what really matters to the customer is not always easy: the ability to "read" a customer's mind is the eventual differentiating factor between a winning and a mediocre business.

Simplicity is about designing easy-to-use products with which customers bond quickly, and providing lucid communication that leaves no room to be mistaken. It is about eliminating whatever complicates the overall offer and overwhelms the customer. In other words, whatever is not understood by the customer or doesn't make the overall experience better should be left out. French writer, Antoine de Saint-Exupéry, summarizes it best: "Perfection is achieved, not when there is nothing more to add, but when there is nothing left to take away."

Have you ever used Apple TV? The product system is composed of a receiver box and a small remote control with three pleasingly contoured buttons. Compare Apple TV's remote control with other models: a carnival of buttons that are dressed up with letters, numbers, abbreviated words and various colors. Take the Apple remote in your hands, close your eyes and try to use it. Can you? Try that with any other remote control. What happens? Apple's fame for its innovative, yet minimalist approach to design and technology is well deserved.

If the customer can use a device (to its full functionality) with her eyes closed, it means that the design is simple. Simplicity is all about getting in and out of the product's world with minimal effort: get the product, use it, benefit from it and move on. Think about it like this: the more you care about the customer, the less the customer needs to be careful about your product.

A seamless frontend requires a "seamful" backend

Seamless experiences require "seamful" backends – "seamful" in the sense that the backends must be interwoven and well-knitted. Simplicity frequently requires complex digital capabilities and flawless integration of business processes. Sometimes simplicity is delivered as an outcome of complex algorithms that run behind an unassuming front-end and project the best-fitting solutions for each customer. Google may be the best example: Google's frontend is an empty text box placed on a white background. Is it possible to have a simpler design for an online search engine? Google's simplicity is only possible due to their technological superiority, which delivers an unparalleled ability to read what is on the user's mind. As the user starts typing (or even beforehand), the complex engine behind the scenes starts producing personalized search suggestions. You may think about it like a mechanical watch: the user sees three simple hands (pointing to the hour, minute and second), while a complex clockwork mechanism, with swings and oscillations, with gears and wheels, works behind to move the hands in harmony with the passage of time. Simplicity is typically produced through an underlying, enabling complexity.

We can conclude the discussion on simplicity by quoting another French writer/thinker, Blaise Pascal, who wrote: "I made this letter longer only because I haven't had time to make it shorter." Take the time to make the customer experience simpler rather than expecting your customers to spend time sorting out your complexity.

(2) Care is a passion, not a fashion

Care is a fashionable topic nowadays. It is fantastic that care is attracting more and more attention from executives. However, treating care like a fashion trend (that is to say, displaying an excessive amount of excitement about it for a limited amount of time before moving on to the next) could result in actions that quickly fail and disappear without making any meaningful change in the way you do business. Making care part of the culture is a long and demanding process in which only the passionate can succeed.

The early days of start-ups are usually defined by the passion of the founding entrepreneur: the passion to address an unattended customer need or want. Founders usually build and run the initial daily business operations. They know the first customers well. They know the customers' desires and preferences inside and out and they deliver the right solutions. The founder is the incarnation of the business in flesh and blood. As the business grows, more people join the ranks of the business and specialization, that is to say, division of the business into functions, comes into play. The founder becomes the CEO or Chairman: more often than not, she loses personal contact with the customers. The passion that led to the creation of the business disappears. Corporations are born out of the corpses of friendly small businesses – we can call this phenomenon the death of small business – and this can replace the image of an openhearted, genuine business with that of the cold face of a corporation. You may frequently hear original, loyal customers complaining about this change: "It is not the same business I used to know and like. They are big now. They don't care anymore."

 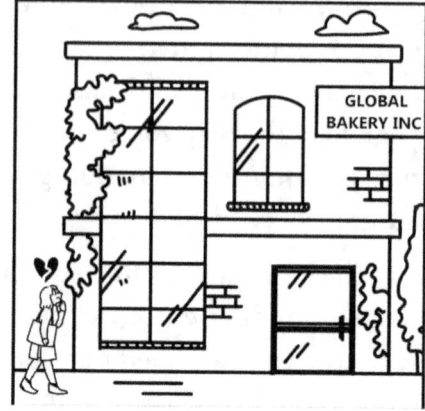

Passion will help you achieve two things: endure the current challenges and develop what the business will become in the future. Passion drives excellence and continuous improvement. It is impossible to deliver an outstanding performance without passion. Humans have complex thoughts, feelings and reactions that sometimes conflict with their previous actions. You cannot successfully interact with humans if you don't have a strong interest in doing so. Moreover, if you aren't feeling strongly about what you do, you cannot reasonably expect others to be passionate about what you produce. The more passionate you are in what you do, the more passionate your customers will be.

(3) Honesty is not optional

In economic transactions, one party (usually the seller) may possess more or better knowledge than the other (usually the buyer) and thereby, is at an advantage in terms of optimizing its transactional benefits vis-à-vis the latter one. This phenomenon is hypothesized under an economic concept known as asymmetry of information. One of the main consequences of the emergence and penetration of internet use is that asymmetry of information is increasingly minimized as a result of increased transparency.

Information is becoming more symmetrical

With just a few clicks, potential buyers are able to evaluate competing products side-by-side, in terms of price and performance, by accessing the readily available information on the price comparison and user review sites. In today's world, honesty is not optional for companies. Hiding a piece of product information (i.e. trying to tilt the information symmetry) is both impractical and unproductive:

- It is impractical because it is impossible to hide anything from the existing users of the product, and the potential buyers have access to the experiences of the existing users. To paraphrase Agatha Christie, the truth has a tendency to reveal itself. This is even more the case in the age of internet and global connectivity.

- It is unproductive because once the truth is known, the backlash will wipe out any short-term benefit achieved through the asymmetry of information. Negative reviews spread more quickly and attract more attention than positive ones. There is no room for hidden surprises anymore. It is better to say no than to make a false promise.

It is difficult to claim that businesses have realized and acted on the shifting equilibrium of information symmetry. The honesty gap, as defined by the difference between what customers expect from businesses and what they observe in terms of sincerity, is wide and omnipresent. Cohn & Wolfe, a communications agency, is researching authenticity based on reputational attributes and publishes the Authentic 100 list (Cohn & Wolfe, 2017). Claimed to be the largest global study on authenticity (covering 14 markets, 1,600 brands and 12,000 consumers), their research reveals that 78% of consumers don't think brands are open and honest. In Western Europe, openness and honesty are a bigger challenge: more than 90% of consumers are found to be skeptical. Below is a snapshot of their research findings:

Customer Agreeing that Brand and Companies...
Percentage of respondents

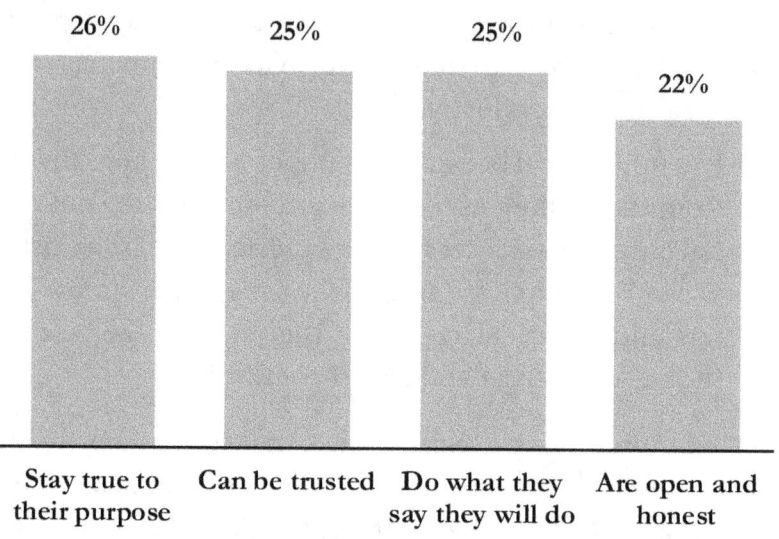

26%	25%	25%	22%
Stay true to their purpose	Can be trusted	Do what they say they will do	Are open and honest

Cohn & Wolfe, The Authentic 100 Research
(Cohn & Wolfe, 2017)

Let's look into some typical drivers of this honesty gap. For instance, when asked about the competitors' products, the typical corporate response is as follows: "as a matter of business principle, we don't comment on competitive products." Why not? There are millions of people out there commenting about your products and comparing them to others. Don't you have enough understanding of the product offering in the marketplace and the user feedback about different products? If your products have an observed weakness, why don't you admit it openly and develop a mitigation plan? For instance, you might admit that your product is more expensive than the others in the market but make a list of your superior features in order to explain your price premium. If you don't have any superior features, your product should not be more expensive than the rest. An unmerited price premium isn't sustainable in the long run. It only takes a second for customers to get a snapshot of value for price through product review websites.

"There is no better way to overpower a trickle of doubt than with a flood of naked truth," Francis J. Underwood, House of Cards (Netflix, 2013)

If you have facts on the superior features of your products, why don't you share them with potential buyers? Sometimes, I see booking.com ratings displayed in hotel receptions. These ratings are produced based on collective input of previous visitors. As a loyal customer of the booking.com website, I trust that these ratings are just general assessments of a hotel. I also trust the quality of the hotels openly displaying their booking.com rating (or any equivalent one). Obviously, only hotels with higher ratings display them. Does it matter? Not displaying a rating, hiding a fact, is an inherent way of accepting low quality. By the way, I also have the habit of comparing the displayed rating with the actual one on the booking.com website and warning the hotel staff whenever I discover a discrepancy.

Every company should compile the reviews from publicly available sources and share them with its frontline (customer facing) staff on a regular basis. Your staff should be as informed as your current and potential customers about the external reviews your products have received – both positive and negative. Otherwise, you could be facing an information asymmetry challenge: your customer would know better or more than your frontline employees. Not commenting on the competitive products doesn't make you principled: it makes you shady. Commenting in an unbiased and fact-based manner would make you a knowledgeable and trusted partner. You should in keep in mind that disparaging competitive products, blindly praising your own products or hiding critical information can quickly cause erosion of trust. It takes only a few clicks to discover many counterstatements to yours. More importantly, we all know that customers trust those counterstatements (made by other customers) more than your own statements. Therefore, it is better to accept the weaknesses in the first place and make a plan to fix them. Bottomline, no product has absolute superiority over all its competitors. Have you ever heard of a product with 100% share in a multi-product market with no competitive restrictions? It is all about being better than the others in some aspects: the more aspects, the better, obviously.

Making pricing and contractual terms open and honest is a must these days. I remember receiving an offer from an insurance company fifteen years ago which consisted of ten different car insurance packages. Actually, instead of trying to understand my preferences in terms of insurance parameters, they dumped all of the available packages on me, expecting me to sort out my own problem. I assume that by complicating the decision-making process, they were expecting customers to pick the most elaborate (overpriced) package, as human beings are risk-averse in nature. Instead of taking any uncovered risk, people are usually ready to pay a premium for the sake of peace of mind. However, I took a piece of paper and mapped out all the packages against parameters like coverage scope, maximum insured amount, initial waiver and service options. I identified the basic coverage, common across all options, and what additional elements were offered in each package. Thereafter, with the help of basic mathematical modeling, I decoded their pricing structure: how the insurance price varies with the different insurance parameters as well as the implied discount for bundled options. I selected the policy that offered me the best value for money based on my perceived likelihood of certain risks happening. After being through a complex decision-making process, I was self-trained on insurance policy selection.

I think that the insurance industry has probably suffered the most from increasing price transparency. Nowadays, pricing comparison sites are a few clicks away. These sites present insurance prices and coverage options from different companies in a simple comparison table format. It only takes another click to request a contractual offer following a quotation. Today's customers don't need to go through the same hassle as before. The asymmetry of pricing information has been pretty much eliminated.

Last year, I called my insurance company to cancel my existing contract. They asked me why. I told them that I found a cheaper offer. They eventually matched the competing price in order to retain my business. Insurance companies could still take advantage of the fast-shrinking group of customers who don't or can't use price comparison sites or a tiny group of customers who have no/limited price sensitivity. However, if you are selling a commoditized product, what could you offer me to justify your price premium? For instance, facts on your claim response rate? Presumably. However, I haven't yet seen an insurance company with strong communication in that area.

Collective expertise of the crowds

I also remember the days when wine companies were heavily using image-based pricing. Selecting a good bottle of wine is an expert task as there are so many variables, such as grape types, producers and year of production. Wine companies routinely overpriced mediocre wines to take advantage of one basic consumer assumption: the more expensive a product is, the higher the quality. Consumers of this overpriced wine were frequently unpleasantly surprised by the quality of the product when they finally opened the bottle. Those days are over. Wine apps are now frequently used: when you scan a bottle (or go through the hassle of writing its full name), these apps offer you a full review. For any grape type, you can sort the wine based on price and consumer ratings. Connectivity is empowering customers in a way that eliminates decision-making complexity and takes away the advantage of those who were previously in the know. This phenomenon can be called the collective expertise of the crowds.

There are also good examples of transparency. For instance, Nordstrom openly communicates their pricing policy to the general public on their website. They accept the fact that discount retailers may offer the same product at a lower price. However, they also provide assurance that they are committed to offer the best possible price among the national department store chains. Moreover, they offer their customers the right to request price adjustment if the price of a purchased item is reduced within 14 days after purchase. This clearly defined and openly communicated policy helps address pricing-related worries that Nordstrom customers may have and gives them peace of mind while shopping at Nordstrom. This is good caretaking.

Table 3. Nordstrom's Pricing Policy

Competitor Price Matching

We are committed to offering you the best possible prices. If you find an item that we offer, in the same color and size, in stock at a designated national competitor, we will gladly meet that competitor's price.

We are unable to match prices from outlet, discount, flash sale, auction or club websites, or from regional or non-U.S.-based stores and websites. Other retailers' promotional discounts, gift card or shipping offers are also not eligible for matching.

Nordstrom Sale Adjustment

If we permanently reduce the price of an item you purchased, we will happily adjust the sale price at your request within 14 days of your shipment date. The item must be the same color and size and must be in stock.

Honest language

Honesty is not only about what you say, but it is also about how you say it. Honesty requires speaking the same language as the customer. As human beings, we all feel more relaxed when we engage in a natural dialogue in a friendly environment. This relaxation is critical for customers to voice their real desires. Only at that moment, when we discover what the customer is really in need of, can we provide better care and thereby, secure a better perception of the brand.

For instance, in direct customer interactions, employing an excess of legal language in order to cover even the most remote legal risks, would alienate customers and destroy their trust. Avoiding marketing nonsense is also critical. In almost all jurisdictions, marketing claims should be true, accurate, not misleading or deceptive, and be supported by solid scientific facts or fact-based research. As a result, a double-play of legal and marketing jargon is commonly observed: a marketing claim is often followed by a legal disclaimer. In direct customer interactions, this may be the best way to kill trust before it grows.

(4) Valuable only if relevant

In a customer's dictionary, value equals relevance. Each product is a solution designed to be relevant by addressing a need. The existence of a product is valuable only if it is relevant to the customer. Obviously, relationships are not built by careless actions, such as spamming the customers with irrelevant promotional offers on slow-moving products. Relationships are built on finesse. Ask yourself: do you have customer finesse?

Customer finesse, or relevance, can be summarized as the right communication, the right offer, at the right time and in the right channel. Being right requires being in the know. That is to say, knowing what is going through your customer's mind, his predicaments and anxieties. The better you know your customer, the better you are positioned to give the care he wants when he needs it.

For instance, I recently came across a wonderful advertising campaign by a computer brand. They were promoting one of their most sophisticated laptops as the "ultimate gaming computer." They were running these commercials at the end of the school year on youth-oriented TV channels and radio stations. This gaming device was positioned to attract the attention of gaming-oriented youth right as their summer vacation was about to start. But the great act of care that stood out was the full refund they were offering in case a user struggled to load and play any off-the-shelf game on the computer. This shows that they understood what might go through the user's mind.

His biggest anxiety: failure to load and play a game. They took care of this anxiety with a full refund offer.

The right offer:

In today's marketplace, selling is an act of understanding the needs and wants of a specific customer in order to proffer the right solution. Hopefully, that solution involves one of your products. In general, sales skills are evolving from assertive to receptive: from persuasion and pitching to active listening and problem solving. Businesses should focus on finding solutions for customers, not customers for solutions. Cross-selling (i.e. selling a related product) and upselling (i.e. selling a more advanced and usually more profitable product) are trendy topics which attract a lot of executive attention. However, blind tele-marketing and e-mail marketing (that is to say, not personalized, not at the right moment) are passé.

One frequently debated matter is whether sales can actively be pushed by the service personnel. The answer is that sales could be pushed in this way, but only if selling is properly positioned as delivering a service for the customer. The service should result in identifying a relevant solution. It is important to keep in mind that using service as a pretext for sales can erode trust and harm the relationship. Service personnel, assuming that they are incentivized for sales, should not follow their blind ambition to pursue revenue or other goals at the expense of service. The approach should be to perfectly execute the service to create mutual trust and unearth customer needs before attempting to sell through a personalized offer that addresses a specific customer need.

Think about a customer who is unhappy with his internet connection speed at home or the data usage limit on his mobile phone. An upgraded subscription package would address the customer's needs. However, such a package will come at a higher cost to the customer. Product advisory, which aims to find the most appropriate solution for the customer, is the right approach in terms of sales as a service. The best solution would be the one that could offer the customer a better subscription while not causing an increase in total cost. The first step in identifying the solution would be to understand the current subscription services used or needed by the customer and his family. The second step would be to do a fit and gap analysis between the customer's needs and the various packages offered by the business. Maybe the best solution is a bundle package that combines the home internet, cable TV and fixed-line telephone into one subscription. Maybe it is a family package which includes multiple mobile phone subscriptions. Maybe it is a mega package that combines all these products together. For the customer, it would be advantageous to enjoy better communication solutions for the same or lower price. For the telecom operator, it is desirable to be the sole provider of communication services for the whole family. This is a typical win-win situation that can be achieved if the business positions itself as a trusted advisor to the customer.

Sometimes, the right offer is not something you sell, but one of your auxiliary products: for instance, a shopping bag. Premium retailers are increasingly investing more in nice, solid bags.

The longer the customer carries the bag and the more he reuses it, the more he promotes that brand free of charge. That is great news. However, as a customer in the middle of a shopping trip, going from one store to another, what annoys you the most? Obviously, all the various sized bags you need to somehow carry in your hands. Whenever you see a customer whose hands are full of bags, why don't you offer him a large bag in which he can put as many of his other bags as possible? It is a great act of care and a chance to maximize your visibility while decreasing the visibility of all the other brands. I have experienced this before. The exact question the sales assistant asked was: "Shall I give you a large bag so that you can put all your stuff together?" I replied: "I could not want anything more at this moment." I felt warmth.

Sometimes, the right offer is not to offer anything, instead of offering something useless. I believe many of us have experienced issues with our gym's accounting department. At least, I have. I don't know why but accounting geniuses never end up working for gyms. Anyway, I joined a new gym and they offered me a free private training session during enrollment. I have never used that option as I don't see the value of a private training session, even if it is free of charge. Yet, three months after joining, they charged my credit card for a private training session. I notified their accounting team and requested the fee to be recredited. I received an explanation that the private training session was mandatory for all new members and the charge was automatic. It was rather shocking to hear this from the accounting team, rather than the client relationship representative who enrolled me. Plus, a full ten points for the transparency on terms and conditions! After a ton of frustrating back and forth communication, I managed to have the fee recredited. However, I was openly annoyed. A few days later, I received a phone call from their head of customer relations. He apologized for the incident and offered me a free private training session, which, I assume, is their standard goodwill offer. Great! Something that I didn't want in the first place, which was offered to me and caused problems later, was reoffered to me. I didn't know what to say: my frustration was reignited.

The right communication:

What is the first thing that your customer needs to know in a given moment along his journey with you? OK, now what are the second and third? Everyone in your company should be able to answer these questions by heart, and if the answers are consistent across the organization, it is a sign of a business unified by a common vision of developing customer-relevant solutions.

Many businesses operate with the incorrect assumption that any interaction with a customer is an opportunity to promote their products. It is not! Any interaction is an opportunity to make a good impression. However, many times, using an unrelated interaction to promote your products increases the risk of making a poor impression.

Think about someone calling an airline helpdesk to rebook his ticket as his original flight is canceled. No one likes bad surprises: to wake up, turn on their phone and receive a flight cancelation message. The customer cannot possibly be in a great mood when she calls. While waiting for the next available agent, she is forced to listen to the tagline that is being continuously repeated: "Welcome to the world's best airline, the winner of this year's Skytrax award." Really? Who cares? Think about the amplifying frustration as the waiting time gets longer. No airline is going to be seen as the world's best at that moment. That communication is counterproductive: it is like pouring gasoline on a fire at a time when success depends on extinguishing the fire as quickly as possible.

Designing customer-relevant communication requires a deep understanding of key functional pain-points and their criticality on the customer experience in order to develop proactive solutions. Think about hearing the "your call is important to us, thank you for waiting" statement for 15 minutes. As the waiting time increases, so does the frustration. If my call is so important, why don't you pick up the darn phone? Such a statement clearly misses sincerity. Why not try being honest? Why not share some useful information with the customer? Put yourself in the customer's shoes and think about what you would like to know if you were in their place: Estimated wait time? The time of the day when lines are less busy? Other service options?

Take the example of my friend who just bought a new coffee machine. It has a simple design with a few buttons. Yet it came with a 16-page manual. My friend wanted to try her new machine immediately, but didn't want to go through the manual. Just put yourself in her shoes. As a new user, she probably had three immediate questions in mind:

(1) Does it need any assembly?

(2) How much coffee do I need for one cup of coffee?

(3) How do I get the machine going?

She had to rush through 16 pages to get answers to these three basic questions. Imagine the excitement of the new product purchase being replaced by the frustration of having to study a manual. A company that cares about its customers should avoid this situation. You need to anticipate the first few questions that are likely to appear in the mind of a first-time purchaser. Then you need to develop a simple communication method to address these questions before they even pop up in the customer's mind. Here is one solution: a sticker on the start button that says "press here to start," another sticker that says "no assembly necessary" and a permanent print on top of the machine depicting in a graphical manner that one spoon of coffee equals one cup. Thereafter, your customer can start enjoying her new machine without losing her excitement. More importantly, when she sees those stickers and graphics, she will feel warmth towards your brand because her entry into use of the product was made easy.

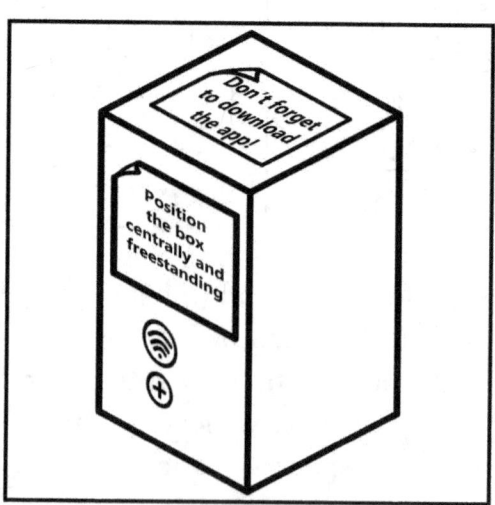

Finally, here is a positive personal experience. I recently received a new generation internet box from my service provider, which is supposed to improve the internet connection speed and allow me to benefit from improved service. The box was elegantly designed: it was a white device that came wrapped in a transparent film. As I unwrapped the film, I saw two simple graphics: one indicating that I should position the box centrally while leaving it freestanding (for an optimal reception), and the other showing that I should download the user app to benefit from all the additional features. The company had highlighted the two most important points that the customer needs to know in order to get the most out of their product. It effectively communicated these points with the help of relevant and valuable visual aids, which quickly attract the attention of customers as they unwrap the product. This is an example of communication that is more relevant than any commercial messaging such as "the most advanced internet technology" or "welcome to the internet of the future."

The right time:

Help is most valuable when it comes at the right time. For instance, a life raft arriving just when you are about to drown in the open sea. Thankfully, in business, problems are usually less severe than drowning. However, timing still matters. We should engage with customers at their preferred time, not ours. We are used to sales assistants jumping on us as soon as we enter a store, asking whether we need any help. They spam us, so to speak, with their offer to help and usually disappear right afterwards. They are never around when you really need some help later. This is a careless tick-the-box exercise. Help is only really valuable at the right time and place. Sales assistants would serve me better if they told me where I could find them when I need help. It is possible to time your support offer well by being anticipative rather than reactive. It is not difficult to identify someone who is puzzled: just watch for the facial expressions or hesitant gestures. That is right time to ask if the customer would like some help.

If you have ever played soccer, one of the first pieces of advice you probably heard from your trainer was that timing is what matters most when going for a header. The ball and your head should meet at the right moment. If a customer interaction is initiated by you, the timing of the contact becomes as important as the timing of a header. The best time to interact is when the customer is doing nothing and is bored. Reaching out to a customer when he is occupied with more important stuff - and believe me, people have tons of other things in their lives more important than your product - will not get you the attention you are looking for. It may even irritate the customer if your attempt comes at a really bad time.

It is difficult to establish general rules regarding the best days of the week or the best times of the day to reach out to a customer. We all operate on different daily schedules. However, the better you know your target audience, the better assumptions you may make. For instance, commuting hours (early mornings and late afternoons) are a good choice for the salaried workers using public transportation. They are likely to be more receptive to written communications during this period of the day. For the salaried workers commuting with their own car, a verbal communication could be more relevant, assuming that they have a handsfree option. On the contrary, early mornings and late afternoons are pretty poor choices to contact stay-at-home mothers as they are usually busy taking their children to and from school. Occupation, gender, as well as cultural differences play a great role in selecting the right time: in some cultures, taking care of personal tasks during work hours is not particularly well-viewed. In others, people have more willingness to get over with less critical personal conversations during worktime rather than wasting their valuable free time. If you have to a make a wild guess regarding the contact time in the absence of any meaningful insights, then try the early afternoon slot: 1:00-3:00 PM. People are usually busier in the mornings and evenings. Additionally, people are usually happier after lunch. For many of us, lunch is an important milestone in the day, marking the halfway point. Many times, businesses have to initiate their engagement with little knowledge and broad assumptions. However, as they increase the level of knowledge about the profile of their target audience, they should optimize both the time and channel of engagement in order to increase the probability of a successful reach out.

The right channel:

As there is a whole chapter devoted to channels, we probably don't need another extended discussion here. In brief, the right channel is the one that your customer feels the most comfortable with for a specific interaction. Therefore, the most suitable channel is both customer and interaction dependent. The same customer may prefer a face-to-face channel for purchasing and a remote channel for product screening. Moreover, we shouldn't immediately assume that the preferred channel will always be a modern, technologically fortified one. Some of your customers may prefer fax! Take, for example, an elderly Japanese customer. You might be laughing, but this is not a small demographic group: almost a third of the Japanese population is above 60 and they are mostly comfortable with fax. There is frequent media coverage on the affection to fax in Japan, one of the most technologically advanced countries in the world. While the Smithsonian is adding a fax machine to its collection as an artifact in the US, the Japanese are still buying millions of fax machines each year. The distrust against transferring personal information on the internet, the desire to create a paper trail of orders, the warmth of handwritten fax notes and limited adeptness with keyboards (especially among the older Japanese) still render fax machines relevant in Japan. So, many Japanese seem to prefer keeping the tried-and-true ways. Now, all this may seem like an urban legend. It seemed to me too until I oversaw the installation of tens of fax machines in order to be able to offer service in a channel that many in Japan still feel comfortable with.

Relevance requires staying current

Relevance requires staying up to date with customers. Spending time where your customers spend time, such as retail stores or contact centers, will help you observe what is going on in their minds. Data collection and analytics will allow you to identify customer trends. We are living in a fast-evolving world; customers constantly expect product improvement and novelty. Businesses are under pressure to innovate and keep up with the competition. However, it is important to note that:

- Novelty is expected, but innovating for the sake of flooding the market with something new doesn't work. Features and functionality are valuable only if they are relevant to customer desires. What customer problem does the new product address or what will it improve in terms of customer experience? You shouldn't add a new feature just because you can. Or even worse, because a brilliant jerk in your organization wants to earn credit for action orientation and (useless) creativity.

- Understanding what other players in the industry are doing is critical, but there is no reason to be obsessed with their actions or try to gain parity by jumping on the bandwagon. Are you sure that they are able to read what is on your customer's mind better than you can? If you are playing to win, you should do better than them. The excellence of competition shouldn't be your limiting factor in customer finesse.

(5) In it for the long haul

Have you ever visited the Grand Bazaar in Istanbul? If you haven't, you should. It is truly an amazing experience. In order to attract the attention of visiting tourists, handicraft sellers shout, "Come over, I will take your money," meaning, "I will make you an offer that you can't reject." It is a remarkable example of hit and run business: they rely on the low likelihood of the same tourist visiting their shop ever again. If your business has a hit and run strategy, you don't really need to care about building a long-term relationship. Just focus on your one-hot offer. Otherwise, you need to make your customers believe that purchasing a product from your business or, even before that, becoming aware of your brand is the beginning of a long mutual journey.

Here is an example of how a long-term buyer-seller relationship started for me. I was buying a laptop from a large electronics retailer. I was in between two models: an expensive model with higher processing capabilities and a more affordable model with lower performance. I asked the sales assistant about the two models. The expected reaction in such a situation is that the sales assistant will gush about how great the more expensive model is and try to upsell. But he did not. Instead he asked what I would be using the laptop for. I explained to him that I only needed it for Microsoft Office and internet. He immediately advised me to buy the cheaper product, noting that he would only recommend buying the more expensive model if I were a graphic designer or playing online virtual reality games. I bought the cheaper product. This may sound like a bad sales practice. However, it is definitely a good practice in care: understanding and developing solutions that best address the customer need. At that particular transaction, the retailer made less money; but they earned my trust. Since then, I have purchased all my electronics from this store. I have a presumption that their sales assistants are knowledgeable and trustworthy as a result of this one experience. In the alternative scenario, I could have bought the more expensive laptop after being convinced to do so by the sales assistant. I could have regretted paying a lot for something that I did not need and that regret could have caused me to never go back to that store. As human beings, we tend to distance ourselves from regret because regrets are the root of unhappiness.

It is reckless for a business to sacrifice long-term prosperity for the sake of short-term gains. Here is another great quote from Antoine de Saint-Exupéry: "It is only with the heart that one can see rightly; what is essential is invisible to the eye." Eyes see what is readily available in your physical proximity. To see what is further away in both time and distance, you need to use your heart. This is equivalent to putting yourself in the shoes of customers while taking a business decision or making an intervention. Actually, we are all customers: we are business representatives of one product, but customers of many products. We are more experienced at being a customer than we are at representing a business interest. However, when it comes to business, we do not always use this experience; we wear a different hat. Don't wear that hat! Keep your customer hat on! Do what you are most experienced at and do what your heart and your expertise as a customer tell you to do.

Lack of care in packaging is an example of what can happen when the heart is missing in business decisions. I was a regular drinker of a carbonated soft drink, consuming three or four cans a day. I bought my weekly consumption need in bulk: a pack of 24 cans, wrapped together in an unbranded, frustratingly weak, see-through packaging. Each time, I had difficulty handling the 24-packs as the outer packaging was not strong enough to carry the weight of 24 full cans and, to top it off, there was no handle. One day, things went catastrophically wrong. The outer packaging ripped as I was taking a 24-pack from my car's trunk. It dropped on the cement and landed right where the cans open up. This was the worst way the pack could have landed and caused the maximum damage: half of the cans popped open. It was a mess to clean up and to separate the good cans from the damaged cans. Thereafter, I did not stop drinking the beverage – it is still my drink of choice. However, I stopped buying the 24-pack. I run out of stock more frequently and perhaps even subconsciously enjoy running out because I force myself to drink fizzy water instead. My Customer Lifetime Value for the brand has diminished significantly since this disaster.

I am pretty sure that the executive who likely came up with the genius idea to save a cent by weakening the outer packaging of the 24-pack saw dancing dollars in front of his eyes: he may have reported in his year-end performance review the great savings he achieved in the year of implementation. One might claim that the thinner plastic packaging was introduced as a more environmentally-friendly solution. I don't buy that claim because, if that were the case, then why were their branded plastic formats excessively thick? Moreover, why do they still use plastic wrapping rather than the easier-to-recycle carton packaging?

You may think that a simple accident and some weak plastic wrapping triggered these thoughts because I am overly vested in the subject. You may think that someone less involved in the topic, pretty much any other customer, would not think that deeply about the matter. You are so mistaken. Customers have very strong instincts: whatever is going on in your company will invariably be sensed from outside. This is great news, actually, because if you act positively on behalf of your customers, they will notice your good deed.

The secret to building a long-term relationship is hidden in this formula:

Personal touch + Inclusion + Transparency + Patience =
Long-term relationship

The more faith your customers have in your honesty and business acumen and the more openly you communicate, the more confidence they will have in the solutions (products) you offer them and the longer they will stay with you. Personal touch, inclusion, transparency and patience are the most critical ingredients for building a long-term relationship.

Personal touch:

In today's connected world, we are all mini celebrities. We are increasingly self-centered, believing that we are very important. We post photos of what we ate for lunch on social media, believing that there are people out there who are excited to know about it. The scale of our feeling of being celebrated is proportional to the size of our social media network. We all feel unique, so we all want and appreciate special treatment in line with our uniqueness.

Personalization of interactions, offers and service according to customer's individualities make up one facet of personal touch. How do you feel when you receive an e-mail that starts with "Dear Madam/Sir?" Do you feel special when the sender doesn't care to know who you are? Do you feel any warmth? How do you feel when you call a helpdesk and the service agent picks up the call by saying, "Hello Mrs. Shaw. How can I help you today, madam?" Or when the service agent asks whether you are happy using a product you purchased a year ago? Or when she informs you about the promotions and limited-edition products available only online as she realizes that you haven't logged into the brand's website in the last twelve months? You may feel a bit like you're being watched by Big Brother. There is probably a tipping point at which you think that they know too much about you. Nevertheless, the feelgood "they know me well" sentiment will usually dwarf any "Big Brother is watching you" anxiety. Your need for being recognized (like a celebrity) will be satisfied. A phone number recognition capability that retrieves the customer profile and interaction history or a CRM system that recommends proactive actions as the interaction flows is all it takes to create a personal interaction for the customer. But it works big-time.

Frequently, businesses invest in personalization through data analysis up to the point of purchase in order to lure potential customers into buying their products. However, the same level of effort often doesn't go into planning the post-purchase interactions. It should. Keep in mind that existing customers are more valuable (financially) than potential customers. Progressive information collection in each interaction is obviously critical as small details allow you to communicate with your customers in a way that makes them feel that you know them as a person. Note every piece of information, however small of a detail it may be, as it comes up during natural dialogue.

Personification is an equally important but mostly undervalued facet of personal touch. It is about portraying your business as a living, evolving organism – painting it as a human, with personality, goals, strengths and weaknesses. Refer to your business like a person in your communications. People have a tendency to trust and forgive (the mistakes of) other people, especially the beloved ones, more than they trust and forgive businesses. Consequently, the more your business comes across a person, the more you are likely to benefit from this human-to-human tolerance.

Personification is also about showing the real people behind the business. An effective way would be to feature stories on your website about the employees and their hard work to develop and deliver real solutions for the customers; this helps customers to think about a business as a friend rather than a faceless company.

Inclusion:

Making customers a part of your brand and its progression, enjoying today and developing the future together, can increase personal connection. The goal is to include your customers in the journey of your brand and business in general, so that they are as invested in your success as they would be if you were a friend. A few examples of inclusive actions are listed below:

- **Staying in touch:** It helps to inform customers about the important initiatives that are being undertaken by your business. This should be done in a way in which you share your excitement and enthusiasm about a specific initiative, rather than spamming the customer with every piece of company news. Let them hear it from you, rather than from other sources. Initiatives with major subsequent impact (such as entering into a new business area) or social responsibility aspects are likely to attract your customers' attention. In this regard, Nordstrom sets a good example with the "Nordstrom Cares" initiative and associated communication: Nordstrom's website features many stories about their efforts in community support and reducing their ecological footprint.

- **Stories about long-term customers:** Featuring stories about your most loyal customers on your website or print communication helps to exemplify the type of relationship you'd like to build with all your customers.

- **Asking for friendly feedback:** Businesses frequently ask for feedback from customers, although it is questionable whether they act on this feedback or not. But more importantly, the feedback is often asked in a standard questionnaire format: a generic form with no human touch. Try to find occasions to ask for feedback in human language. For instance, after successfully helping a customer on the phone, your service agent could ask the customer whether she would have time to check your new website and share her opinion. Your agent can offer the customer a means to reach her directly afterwards: a friendly chat, not a structured feedback session.

Yet such an engagement gives the customer more sense of belonging compared to a box-ticking survey.

- **Loyalty programs:** Incentivizing desired behaviors could help build a long-term relationship if done properly. Your loyalty program shouldn't be based on short-term benefits and a this-for-that type of scheme. It should cover all aspects of the relationship, not only one. Points for spending is the most classic loyalty scheme and falls short in building an in-depth relationship or bonding. It is very transactional and easy to replicate. At any given time, another business could offer more points for the same amount spent and lure your customers away. The idea should be to build a multi-layered, complex loyalty program that protects your business, somewhat similar to the city walls protecting the settlements in the Medieval times. The more fortified the walls, the less likely the residents to leave or the nonresidents to enter. As much as possible, every interaction in the customer lifecycle should be incentivized: visiting your website, downloading your app, registering to your e-mail list, recommending a friend, joining an event, staying with your business for a number of years, completing a survey, following your social media account or spontaneously posting something (positive) about your brand.

Transparency:

Businesses usually look like a black box to customers – their inner workings are opaque. However, increasing transparency in your operations and giving your customer a peek of what goes on behind the scenes is a good way to strengthen your relationship: humans tend to dislike the things they don't understand. Trade secret aside, transparency on anything else is appreciated, especially if it is customer-relevant. For example, have you noticed that open kitchens are a growing trend in the restaurant industry? It's because the transparency reassures the customers. Moreover, it is intriguing to watch your meal being made.

"This is our company policy" is an excuse frequently heard by the customers. It is probably the one that amplifies the frustration of the customer the most. Attributing your incapacity to help, that is to say, hiding behind company policies, neither solves the customers' issues nor creates any sympathy on your account. However, assuming your company policies are made with people in mind and they aren't all one-sided, explaining the justification behind a policy in human language might offer some clarity to your customers and increase the likelihood of their buy-in. As mentioned above, policy is a term that can have negative connotations in customers' minds. Policy is neither a divine act nor a law; it is something that is decided on within the company. Instead of hiding behind your policies, explain the benefits of your policies to your customers; demonstrate how your policies ensure that you treat every customer the same way and guarantee the same high level of attention to everyone at all times.

Another important area of transparency is what you do with customer feedback. All businesses ask for feedback – often more frequently than is appreciated by customers. But what happens thereafter? It is a complete black hole as far as the customers are concerned. Follow up with customers who have given feedback and demonstrate, whether on your website or through other communication channels, the actions you have taken based on the comments you have received: this simple action helps to demystify the feedback loop. This would not only improve the response rate and quality of responses to your future feedback requests, but also improve the sense of belonging among your customers.

Patience:

Relationships require patience, not in the sense of ability to wait, but in the sense of demonstrating persistence in good behavior without rushing into an end result. Patience is about walking on the right path even if you don't know if and when you will get there. Focus on building a relationship rather than closing a sale. Remember, not all of your customer communication should be focused on selling something, especially when the relationship is not well-established yet. For instance, troublingly, we come across businesses which randomly ask for referrals from people on their mailing lists without knowing who on that list actually uses and enjoys their products. This is a desperate act of lead generation and, most of the time, results in more unsubscribing members than leads.

Tailor and diversify your communication and offer according to the lifecycle stage of your customers. For instance, with new customers, it is valuable to remind them about any product functionality or feature that they aren't using or the benefits of registration to your brand programs. In case you have prospects (potential customers) who are aware of your products and haven't purchased anything from you yet, try to understand their actual needs and why your products have failed to attract them, rather than continuously spamming them with different variations of the same offer. Relationships have stages and you have to progress through these stages sequentially. Sometimes relationships move fast and, sometimes, they don't move at all. But, irrespective of the speed, you need to be patient at all times.

(6) Always there for you

Customers are always on; so from the beginning of the customer journey, your care should always be on too. Moreover, you should assume that this will be an everlasting journey. Starting with helping potential customers find the right solutions, make sure that your reassuring, unassuming shadow follows your customers, watching their back and being ready to jump in whenever needed.

How will you ensure this 24/7 attention day in and day out? This doesn't necessarily mean that you should have a service center operating 24/7. Instead, it is about enriching your care options and ensuring that at least one self-sufficient interaction channel is available at all times for every possible support need and customer profile. This could mean that you:

- build online or in-person communities for your customers to learn from and support each other

- make AI-powered digital solutions available to facilitate self-service

- equip the web with how-to videos, posts or any other type of knowledge articles

- put in place a continuous learning program to keep your customers up to date regarding what is moving in and around your industry and products

In every relationship, there will be good times and bad times, and your actions in the bad times will determine what type of business you are. Customers may not always be right or reasonable, but they always deserve your utmost care. You will often face angry customers; however, your consistent calmness will cool them down. Your ability to accommodate poor behavior, up to an impossible point, will be seen as a virtue and will increase personal affinity with your brand. The relationship may also reach the point of termination. How well are you prepared to counsel your customers out? Do you offer contractual flexibility to your customers? How easy is it for your customers to modify or cancel their subscriptions and contractual terms? Easy subscription and difficult termination are a form of dishonesty. Don't forget that counseling out may be your last chance to make a good impression: make it easy and offer advice on other possible alternatives. Ultimately, this is a two-way street: whoever quits today may come back tomorrow if he can't find what he was looking for elsewhere. It is always better to end the relationship on a positive note.

Netflix is a great example. Canceling is even easier than subscribing. You press a button and you are out. Yes, afterwards, you receive the "we are sorry to see go" and "come back" messages. However, seeing those messages isn't frustrating after a painless separation experience. Actually, you might even feel kind of guilty. Ease of cancellation is surely one of the main drivers of Netflix's global subscription growth.

Agility for the unexpected

Being agile for the expected is old news and no longer meets the expectations of today's customers. Your policies will cover the expected. The key question is how to be ready for the unexpected. Your ability to weather the unexpected depends on how you recruit, train and empower your people. As your people handle the unexpected through creative solutions, make sure to keep track. Record all unexpected situations and requests faced and develop standard solutions for them in order to be ready for the next time. Unexpected events train you and improve your capability to deliver. It's okay to break the rules from time-to-time to help customers in desperate circumstances. Your care shouldn't always be capped by company policies: all can be broken on an exceptional basis if it is about making your customer's day. Make customers the priority, not strict adherence to policies, and ensure that your policies aren't written by people who haven't handled a single customer case in their entire lives. Don't forget the shift of power over time. This means your customers will eventually be in charge or control. In the short-run, the issues are more important to your customers and your customers are in a more distressed situation than you are. However, in a competitive market, customers can develop an alternative solution and terminate the relationship with you. Over time, you will end up in a worse situation than your unhappy customers.

(7) We are what we repeatedly do

An outstanding interaction could deliver remarkable delight and grab customers' utmost attention. It could also lead to word-of-mouth referral, albeit being limited in time and impact. However, one outstanding interaction doesn't earn you loyalty. There is no need to do legendary, heroic acts. Do small things, but do them right and consistently. Everyday simple efforts deliver results. Think about spending half an hour exercising every day versus spending five hours exercising three days a month: which one is likely to yield better results in the long run while avoiding injury and burnout?

One of the first things they told me at my first job at a leading management consultancy firm, was, "You may do an extraordinary job in one project and, surely, you will gain credibility. However, that credibility lasts for half an hour. Then, you need to reprove yourself." The relationship with customers is no different. What you repeatedly do matters much more than what you do once. Obviously, product quality and reliability are the most fundamental elements of repetition. In simple terms, your product should work as intended each and every time. It is not easy to develop a long-lasting relationship with a customer if your product delivers what it is supposed to deliver only from time-to-time and not always at the same level.

Win through habits

Both habits and reputation are created through consistency. It is a duality that works in great harmony. Humans form habits through repetition of an act over a long period of time, and familiarity is a generally desired attribute by customers. Once habits are formed, they are both hard to break and contagious. As we have mentioned many times before, in today's digital world, we are all ultra-connected thanks to remote communication means and social media, so habits spread much like a computer virus does. How can you help your customers develop a habit of trusting your brand and using your products? It is a long and effortful endeavor, but one that pays back if you are eventually successful. It is the result of consistent repetition of positive interactions. "Excellence is not an act, but a habit. It is an art won by training and habituation," says Aristotle. So is your reputation.

"They sometimes do a great job, but it is difficult to know if and when." Have you ever heard a recommendation like this? Probably not. No one really recommends an inconsistent solution, even if sometimes it delivers spectacular results. It is more likely that you have heard this phrase in association with a disappointed customer. However, you may have heard this one conveying a more positive sentiment: "It is nothing special, but delivers the basics. It is just fine." Even mediocre but consistent performance trumps one hit wonders when it comes to customer perception.

Care irrespective of time and space

The golden rule is: you care, you care each and every time, regardless of time, space and circumstantial factors. A major source of frustration is the inconsistent information and treatment that customers are exposed to in different touchpoints. Considering the proliferation of interactions and channels in today's world, it is challenging to stay true to your brand promise at all times. For instance, attentiveness is frequently promised by brands, yet it is not uncommon that the same brand quickly replies to e-mails, but never picks up the phone. Similarly, some businesses are attentive to the customers shopping online by offering live support, yet they don't offer the same type of live support for customers struggling with the FAQs or help pages.

Consistency separates the good from the mediocre and can only be achieved through an operational setup in which people and systems function in harmony. Standards, policies, controlling and correcting mechanisms are all enablers of harmony. Consistency shouldn't be left only to a hunch. There are as many styles as there are people. This doesn't mean that we should define strict operating procedures that leave no room for personnel to face the unexpected. However, the boundaries of maneuvering should be defined. Policies should not be carved in stone: they should adapt over time. However, they should always evolve in a manner consistent with the overarching theme – that is to say, your brand promise, which defines the common denominator (the minimal commonalities) in your interactions irrespective of the time and space. Timeliness, usefulness, simplicity. Whatever defines the character of your franchise. There will always be channel-based peculiarities in communication and experience because humans cannot use all their senses in all interaction channels. Yet, peculiarities are peculiarities only if there is a general theme common across all interactions. Otherwise, peculiarity is the norm.

Businesses make promises in their brand communication: each customer interaction is a test to confirm or weaken these promises. Businesses typically promise that they will take care of their customers through easy interactions, simple processes, timely and friendly support, accurate and helpful communication. However, discrepancies observed between the promise and delivery damages the perception of a caring brand. On the flip side, customers recognize the caring brands that consistently live up to their promises. In the end, the businesses that succeed in delivering their promises are those which offer genuine and smart care and follow through with it impeccably; customers see right through unrealized claims of care but reward real acts of caring with loyalty and advocacy.

CHAPTER 5

Care Along the Customer Lifecycle

From the moment a customer makes their first contact with a company, they enter a relationship pattern which can often be predicted. This pattern is called the customer lifecycle, and is representative of the various stages of the relationship that a customer may experience during the extent – however long that might be – of their engagement with that company. In this chapter, we will define the customer lifecycle and map out six core care episodes. You may come across different customer lifecycle stages in other literature. Below is the lifecycle that we will be using throughout this book. The five stages of the customer lifecycle are: Learn, Explore, Buy, Live and Share. These main stages are further divided into substages.

Note: Purchase could further be broken into three stages – Select, Pay, Receive

The main reinforcement in this version vis-à-vis the others is the division of the Share stage into two paths: Advocate versus Criticize and Reconcile. Obviously, companies design their activities with the aim of making their customers happy and triggering positive word-of-mouth. However, in real life, not everything goes as planned: there is a continuous reassessment process going on as customers use your products. Each interaction is a test: you may succeed in a majority of them, but ultimately you may fail once or twice. Sometimes the failure doesn't originate in what you actually do, but in the reality that the competition on occasion may develop faster than you do. What was seen as satisfactory before may become a disappointment over time. The bottom line is that even your once-passionate advocates could turn into critics. Because they are hoping for the best, companies are usually not well-prepared to manage a customer journey with an unhappy ending. This is a major pitfall as one critic causes more damage to your business than the benefit brought on by many advocates.

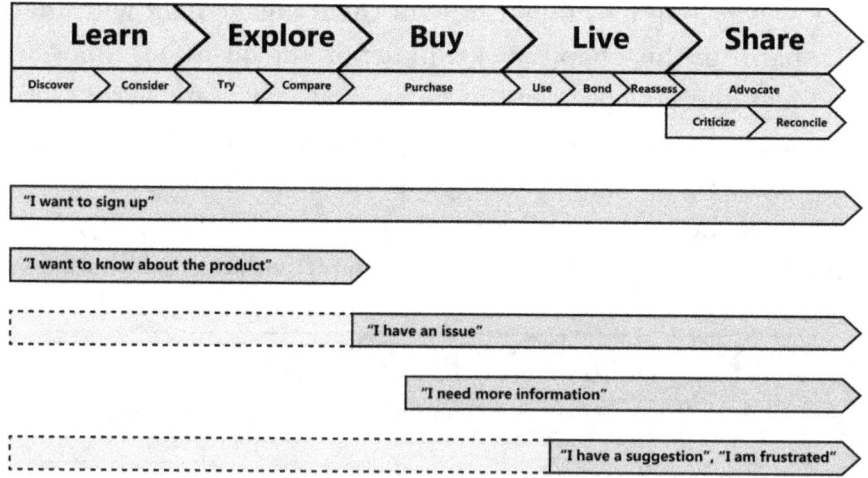

Customer Care plays a critical role throughout the journey, not only after sales

In the previous chapters, we noted that Customer Care should be a core member of the cross-functional team developing the end-to-end customer journey and specifically identified six customer episodes to be safeguarded by the function. In the diagram above, we lay down these six core episodes over the customer journey. Solid lines signify the stages at which the related interactions mainly take place. Dotted lines signify the stages at which some interaction could take place depending on the product characteristics and the commercial model in place. The main message to take away from this diagram is that Customer Care plays a critical role from initial contact to purchase and thereafter: it is not just an aftersales activity.

Episode I: I want to know about the product

The journey starts with the customer realizing that they have a need or want. This realization could be self-triggered as a result of a circumstantial change, such as having more disposable income, moving to a new city or starting a family. It could also be triggered by an external influence, such as a marketing communication that makes the customer feel at a disadvantage by not having a product or owning an inferior product with less functionality (fewer benefits) compared to the other products available in the marketplace. Thereafter, the customer enters into a phase of information collection and processing to understand and review available alternative solutions (products) in order to select the best fit. Customers may resort to commercial communication materials, comparative factsheets, user reviews and expert reviews during the information search phase. They may experience the product through touch and feel, physical demonstrations or risk-free, limited-time trial offers (e.g. one-day free entry to the gym before joining). Eventually, they will compare products according to various dimensions such as functionality, performance, design, price, reliability (risk) and ease of use. They usually make a selection based on maximizing the benefits of purchase.

The depth and length of exploration depends on the product complexity and cost of purchase:

- **Daily consumables:** These are low-cost products that you buy all the time. For instance, chewing gum with a certain flavor would not require much exploration and the usual consumer behavior is to purchase the most readily available product. That is to say, the customer usually purchases the chewing gum displayed next to the checkout counter.

- **Expertise products:** These are low-cost products that are more complicated than everyday purchases. Deciding on which product to buy necessitates a certain level of expertise. You may build this expertise yourself through trial and error. You may also consult the people in the know, the experts. Health and beauty products (such as essential oils, over-the-counter treatments, face creams) and household maintenance items (such as bolts and nuts) are typical examples. Moreover, unique and novel products (new category builders) warrant more elaborate exploration as there is no readily accessible expertise and more customer learning is needed regarding the basics of the product.

- **Rare purchases:** These are big ticket items like laptops, smartphones or automobiles. A lengthy exploration phase usually precedes the purchase. Customers assess all aspects of the product.

The key question is how to position ourselves on the side of the potential customers during the exploration phase. The answer is by being a trusted, impartial partner in their assessment exercise. This is not about glorifying our product in an attempt to motivate potential customers to buy ours instead of another one. This is about helping potential customers to understand all available options and what serves their needs best. I appreciate businesses whose representatives openly say things like, "We are not the cheapest product on the market, but we are certified to be the best in terms of reliability."

All products rely on compromise

There is no omni-dominant product on earth. Products that are superior in terms of functionality and performance are usually more expensive and could be more difficult to use. Customers face a multi-criteria decision-making process: what is the best compromise? Their decision depends on the relative weight of each criterion and varies from one customer to another. Helping customers in the decision-making process should be in the interest of every business. But how? The answer is: by building trust. In most cases, trust sells the product, not the features. Unless the interested customer is an expert (most likely, he is not, as an expert is unlikely to come to you for advice), he won't necessarily have the motivation or technical abilities to make a balanced scorecard type of evaluation. He would be employing a heuristic technique: a mental shortcut, such as intuitive judgement or common sense, to solve the problem even if the result could be suboptimal or imperfect. In most buying decisions, the customer will be looking for others' opinions, in search of a common consensus or to form an intuitive judgement for their case.

In most cases, trust, not the features, sells the product

Why are the user reviews and friends' recommendations more effective than brand communication? Because people trust their friends and peers more. Trustworthy opinions matter more and help customers in developing a mental shortcut. Accordingly, being a companion in product selection hinges on building that trust. The Customer Care function is best positioned to play this crucial role in a business. The Sales and Marketing functions usually have stretch sales targets and, thereby, there is an inherent conflict of interest: it is impractical to act as an impartial, unbiased companion in making a purchase decision when your main functional objective is to promote your own products and increase sales.

Displaying your knowledge and expertise in an impartial manner is the pathway to building trust-based relationships as customers value informative advice. Your ability to do so, at minimum, depends on the availability and accessibility of a knowledge base. A knowledge base is a library of information about your products and services. It should be easily accessible at any point during the customer lifecycle in order to ensure that the customer receives the same information – in terms of both content and quality – regardless of the nature of the touchpoint. In more practical terms, the body of information served to the customer should be the same whether he is reading the FAQs on the website, talking to a service agent over the phone or chatting with a sales assistant in the store. Omnichannel consistency can only be ensured if each and every customer interaction is guided by a regularly updated knowledge base. Ease of retrieving the specific information is a key success factor to complete the ongoing interaction to the full satisfaction of the customer. Today, many cloud-based solutions are available in the marketplace to provide businesses with an anywhere, anytime accessible and searchable knowledge base.

I think the bigger challenge is to properly segment and populate the knowledge base. Knowledge segmentation should be made in such a way as to match the customer's information needs along the journey: segmenting based on the episodes is one smart way to do this. However, for the sake of simplicity, three metalevel knowledge categories could be defined:

(1) *Be Informed:* It covers all the information the customer needs to be able to make an informed purchase decision – in other words, anything that relates to Episode I. This definition stretches beyond your own territory; in order to be a trusted decision partner, your ability to advise should be enriched with unbiased information about your competitors' products and services. Having in place an extensive and updated library of information about the competition is where many businesses fail.

(2) *Enjoy Better:* It covers all the post-purchase information that will help customers make the most out of using your product – anything that relates to Episode III. An idiosyncratic example for this category is how-to-use tips and tricks.

(3) *Resolve:* It covers all the troubleshooting information – anything that relates to Episode IV. Quick issue fixes are the most typical example.

Episode II: I want to sign up

Signing up – the registration of a customer into your database – marks the start of a long journey. Before signing up, the customer knows the brand, at least, to the extent of having some interest in using its goods or services. However, the brand doesn't know the customer. A meaningful relationship is only possible if the two parties get to know each other to some extent. Here, I am not referring to vague segmentations. You may have an idea of the profile of the people using your product: let's say, predominantly aged 25-40, female, married or in a serious relationship, working in an office job. That does not mean that a

50-year old single man, owning a small business, would never use your product. Here, I am referring to knowing the exact individual who has an intention to use your product or is using your product. Tying up the argumentation with the customer - consumer discussion we had earlier in the book, we can conclude that such an in-depth knowledge is extremely precious for companies with strong CRM strategies and capabilities in place.

At the bare minimum, registration requires recording the name, surname and contact information (usually e-mail address) for further correspondence. If possible, having the gender information would ensure proper salutation and some primitive segmentation. We can classify the methods of signing up in three broad categories:

- **Self-registration:** Customers input their information directly to the company's database through a user interface on the website or app.

- **Assisted-registration:** Customer information is inputted by a sales or service assistant in contact with the customer in a face-to-face or remote channel based on the consent of the customer.

- **Automatic registration:** Signing up is a natural consequence of using a product if the product is intended for the use of a designated person. For instance, whenever you open a bank account or buy an insurance policy, you are automatically registered. Shopping online requires registration, unless there is an explicit option of shopping as a guest.

This episode is more relevant to cases where signing up is a triggered need and customers sign up voluntarily and on their own.

Registration symbolizes the birth of a direct relationship

The customer gains identity and transforms from an unknown private individual to a customer. The relationship deepens with each interaction until one side (usually the customer) severs the relationship. In that sense, you may think about your CRM database as a relationship diary. You start with a simple sentence like, "His name is James," and you learn more about him with each event. The better you understand what to look for, the more effective your data collection and processing efforts will be. Favorite color – is that a relevant piece of information? It depends. It is relevant if you plan to communicate via e-mail and you have e-mail templates in different colors. It is relevant if you have a line of physical products that come in different colors. It is irrelevant if you have a mono-color business.

Triggering the need to sign up is a challenging undertaking, especially if the customer can use the product without signing up. For instance, Apple has all its iPhone customers registered as one cannot use an iPhone without an Apple ID. Apple owns both the hardware and the operating system. In contrast, smartphone manufacturers operating on the Android platform don't have immediate access to the same level of information as the bulk of information is collected by Google. These manufacturers try to trigger registration by offering additional benefits such as personalization of the user experience, opt-in for promotional offers, free cloud storage, update notifications, extended warranty, faster troubleshooting and service. This is the typical approach as customers are usually hesitant to share their data and perceive registration as a hassle. Thereby, registration becomes a give and take exercise.

Customer data belongs to the customer

Taking care of customers entails taking care of their data. As customers ourselves, what do we dislike the most about signing up? Lengthy sign up processes, the risk of personal data leakage and subsequent spam e-mails, messages or calls. These issues continuously generate complaints from customers: better care requires eliminating the root causes of complaints. Registration is the entry point and entry barriers should be eliminated or minimized as much possible. Accordingly:

(1) *Simplify the sign-up process:* Large amounts of upfront data requests and unconvincing benefits will lead to low sign-up rates. The most viable approach is to start by asking for the least amount of information possible (such as name, surname and email address) and to progressively collect more data in exchange of incremental benefits over the customer lifecycle. Requested data and offered benefits need to match each other: the more data requested (for a particular future use), the higher the benefits should be.

(2) *Reassure customers about data security:* Explain to the customer how you will protect their data, including any fact-based statements and quantitative metrics on the data collection and storage quality. Having your data protection practices certified by a credible, independent institution is not only a good business practice, but also a source of reassurance for the customer. It is valuable to clearly state with whom the customer data could be shared. Obviously, it would be better if the data were not shared with any third parties; while sharing our personal data, we have a valid concern regarding in whose hands our data will eventually end up. Moreover, humans do like visual communication: using icons of security standards on data treatment in each interaction involving personal data could contribute to this reassurance.

(3) *Reassure the customer about the use of their data:* "Your data for better care" should be at the core of communication. There is nothing wrong with telling the customers that you can take better care of them by knowing them a bit better as long as you deliver on your promise. It is powerful to remind customers that they can opt out from the engagement at any time with one click. Guaranteeing a no-spam policy is helpful in the sense that only relevant content will be shared. Obviously, such a reassurance should only be offered if you trust the predictive strength of your CRM capability.

(4) *Reassure the customer regarding the contact channel:* Make sure to ask customers their preferred contact channel and put in place controls to guarantee that they will only be contacted via that channel. It is important to highlight upfront that potentially more disturbing channels, such as phone calls, will only be used in case of emergency and will not be used for promotional purposes.

Each business should map the potential moments of registration throughout the customer lifecycle in order to develop strategies to increase the overall registration rate and subsequent progressive data collection. This is one of the topics in customer lifecycle management that is frequently taken lightly by businesses. Let's quickly review the different stages of the lifecycle where registration may occur:

- **Learn and Explore:** Potential customers may register at this stage to access exclusive content in order to collect information about a potential future purchase. Some companies offer free or risk-free trials with registration. Another incentive for early registration could be to receive notifications on promotional offers.

- **Buy:** The bulk of registration takes place in parallel to the purchase, either due to the type of relationship imposed by the nature of the product or through incentives. For instance, the customers typically need to register first in order to shop online.

- **Use and Share:** Existing customers may register to have access to service, or to benefit from brand programs such as loyalty schemes or time-limited campaigns.

More regulatory scrutiny on the topic of personal data

Collection and use of personal data are topics which are increasingly attracting more regulatory scrutiny. For instance, the new General Data Protection Regulation (GDPR) went into effect in the EU on May 25, 2018. GDPR standardizes how personal data is stored, processed and exchanged across the member states. It aims to increase privacy for individuals and equips regulatory authorities with more power to proceed against businesses in case of breach. This regulation applies not only to EU companies, but also to all non-EU companies that hold and process the personal data of individuals residing in the EU. According to the GDPR, obtaining consent for processing personal data should be clear, seeking for an opt-in response as opposed to an opt-out response. Individuals are given the right to access their personal data and to be forgotten. They may request a copy of their complete data in an electronic format or deletion of their records at any time. Elsewhere, in the US, private data protection is a more complex subject as there are no overarching regulations. Instead, the US has put in place a set of standards governed by industry-level laws and state-level regulation.

In many companies, ownership of customer data is a topic of internal political struggle. Obviously, all the functions need customer data in order to design their activities. However, it is important to have a single point of accountability for safeguarding customer data. Advancements in the enabling technologies that improve the connectivity and data extraction from each customer interaction result in exponential growth in the amount of customer data being collected on a daily basis. Collection, storage and analysis of a massive amount of data warrants a Chief Customer Data Officer (CCDO) role in data-driven companies within a certain scale. Moreover, according to the EU GDPR, a data protection officer (DPO) should be appointed in these companies.

Leaving aside the ownership of the customer data controversy, I believe Customer Care should safeguard the customer sign-up episode, which is the enabling event for any subsequent data collection. As discussed above, customers may sign up at any time during the lifecycle. Regardless of the sign-up channel, the sign-up process and subsequent account issues drive a large number of inquiries. The Customer Care team needs to master the process in order to handle these inquiries. Moreover, contact centers, usually managed by the Customer Care team, interact with potential and current customers on a daily basis and have instant access to the CRM systems which bring customer data to their fingertips. In many companies, care-related activities generate the largest amount of customer interactions and data. Thereby, the Customer Care team is well suited to facilitate the customer record updates.

Episode III: I need more information

The early days following the first-time purchase of a product (or the onset of the free and risk-free trial period), represent a critical period of time during which the customer faces the bare-naked reality about the product. We can call this period the "honeymoon" phase: it is a period of excitement and discovery. It is also the time when you completely realize that you have passed the "no return after this point" sign in the road. Therefore, it is the moment of truth. First experiences set the tone of the relationship. The key question is: how do you feel at the end of the honeymoon phase? Still happy with what you signed up for? Any regrets? If there are already some regrets despite all the excitement, you should see them as an early indicator for a short-lasting relationship.

You make it or break it during the honeymoon

It is extremely critical for businesses to proactively support their customers during the honeymoon phase. This is especially true if the product is novel or not easy to use and maintain. How does the customer feel a few days after purchase? Confused? Overwhelmed? In control? Pleased? Reassurance is the key: an inner voice should constantly tell the customer that she has made an excellent purchase. How can you plant some seeds in the customer's mind to trigger that inner voice? Through properly designed and executed onboarding to ensure that the customer realizes the full amount of value being offered by your product.

Like any other communication exercise, content and channel are at the core of the onboarding design. In terms of content, the primary objective is to make sure that your customers understand the benefits of your product, how it functions and where they can easily address their questions and issues. It is impossible to truly enjoy any product without really understanding how it works and the benefits. This is critical as no one will promote a product without fully enjoying it.

Create wow with your content

There are two key questions for determining the most customer relevant content: Which product features are appreciated the most by customers? Which product features are understood the least by customers? At the intersection of these two questions lies the bull's eye: the least understood features that would otherwise (i.e. if understood well) be very much appreciated by customers. These features are the ones that would create the wow effect and consequently, your very first onboarding communication should focus on them. This wow effect will increase the likelihood of customers staying interested in the subsequent communication, as it creates curiosity in their minds: "I wonder what else I am missing."

Customers are content hungry, but they want to be in charge of when, where and how to access the content. The style and length of the content are critical as customers dispense with it quickly if it is not engaging/relevant or is simply too long. Short self-learning content, especially if personalized to their needs, is usually attractive.

Testing your customer's product knowledge through gamification is a useful onboarding tool. For instance, put together a test with three questions and send it to your new customers. Obviously, these three questions should be about the three most important things you want your customers to know by heart. The participation rate could be increased by offering a token of appreciation (e.g. a discount coupon or loyalty points) to each customer taking the test.

Prefer content pull over content push as much as possible

In terms of channel selection, unless customers are explicitly open to live verbal communication, written forms (e-mail, or messaging) should be preferred for post-purchase, onboarding interactions, as verbal communication is usually more intrusive to the customer's daily activities. These intrusions could frustrate many customers. It is very likely that your product is not necessarily the most important thing in their lives, so it is best to offer them the flexibility to access your content at their leisure. Moreover, while spoken words fly away, text remains. Customers may need to relook at the text at a later stage: your e-mails and messages will serve as reference documents in that case. Text is also more trustworthy than the spoken word and, if executed properly, does not leave room for confusion. In addition, written communication is less costly and more replicable for companies than spoken communication.

The honeymoon period is the most critical as customers usually have the most questions to ask when new to the product. As discussed, proper onboarding is crucial to put customers on the right track during this critical period. However, this is the beginning, not the end; questions will keep popping up in customers' minds as they use the product. These general inquiries could have to do with anything that relates to your business: campaigns, promotions, loyalty programs, product upgrades, etc. Providing the customer with answers turns into an efficiency game: customers will be looking for speed (ease of access) and accuracy, while businesses will be after cost effectiveness.

Efficiency is best achieved through automated online solutions when servicing is a matter of feeding a diverse set of information to a large number of customers. Any service solution that requires the intervention of service personnel, such as visiting an authorized service point or calling the helpdesk, would be too costly for any business if the sole purpose of the interaction is to satisfy a simple information need of the customer (i.e. if there is no further engagement strategy behind the scenes).

An example from the consumer electronics industry may help the clarify the point. Warranty coverage (duration and scope) of an electronics device is a question frequently asked by customers. Assuming the availability of a proper product tracking system and connectivity between front- and back-end systems, it is possible to retrieve this information in an automated manner and provide it online: customers could log in to their online accounts to instantly check the readily available information or type in the product code to view the warranty information. This solution allows customers to find information when they need it, without consulting anyone. If such a solution weren't available online, customers would have to contact a service provider with access to this information. At scale (i.e. when your business faces thousands of information inquiries), investing in automated solutions pays off quickly. Democratization of information not only improves customer satisfaction, but also decreases the service cost for the businesses.

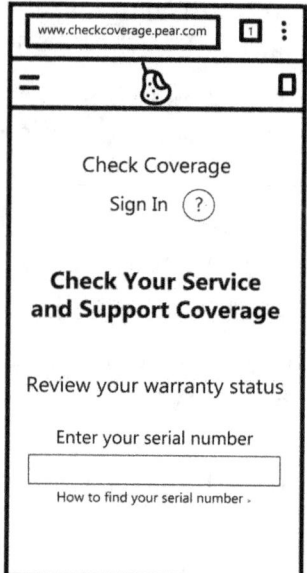

Episode IV: I have an issue

This episode is broadly classified as "customer complaint" in practice: complaint is an expression of dissatisfaction caused by a failure to meet customer expectations. The best way to solve a customer issue is to make sure that the issue does not occur in the first place. However, businesses aren't short of inventing creative ways to fail.

We can categorize the failures in four nonexclusive groups:

(1) *Core functionality failures:* Frequently referred to as product failure, this is about a product not delivering its intended benefits. For instance, let's take the example of dining out, which is a service product. You ordered a medium cooked steak and receive it well-done, or even burned. There is clearly a discrepancy between the expected and actual product delivery. The steak is not delivering what it is supposed to deliver (i.e. juiciness, tenderness and the pinkish color of a medium cooked steak).

(2) *Service failures:* Let's assume that you tried to book the steak restaurant on its website and the booking tool is not working. Or the text message you were supposed to receive to confirm your reservation never arrived. Both are service failures that affect the overall experience, but not the core product delivery (such as the taste of your steak or the ambiance of the restaurant).

(3) *Communication failures:* Let's assume that the waitress recommended the chef's special sauce to go with your steak. Pleased with the recommendation, you included the sauce in your order. However, the waitress forgot to mention the dietary concerns: the sauce is made with regular milk and, as a lactose intolerant person, you started to feel sick after eating the sauce. This is a classical communication failure which frequently results in a discrepancy between the expected and actual product delivery. This is not a core functionality failure as, for a lactose tolerant person, the sauce delivers on its promise. In practice, misunderstandings and overpromising (underdelivering) are the main drivers of communication failures.

(4) *Channel and touchpoint failures:* For instance, ordering food is one touchpoint in the dining experience. A wait-

ress mixing up the orders and coming back to reconfirm your orders is a touchpoint failure. Maybe this is due to the waitress's state of mind not being at its best that evening. You may experience a similar issue even in a technologically-equipped restaurant in which the orders are inputted directly by the customer to the system through the touchscreens integrated at the tables: this time, the problem is presumably a system failure. Despite being carried out in two different channels, it is a failure in the same activity (order taking) irrespective of the underlying driver.

The single most important objective in issue handling is to ensure the continuity of the relationship. It is irrelevant who is right or wrong: customers always have the right to service. No business can benefit from winning an argument with the customer because in the end, you would end up with a customer who is unhappy after losing an argument. There is no need to lecture a customer.

At this point, it makes sense to revisit the Service Recovery Paradox (McCollough & Bharadwaj, 1992). The paradox claims that a customer who experienced an issue (with a service product) and has seen the issue pleasantly resolved through service is likely to exhibit satisfaction and loyalty levels (i.e. repurchase rates) equal to or higher than a customer who hasn't experienced an issue in the first place. The rationale behind this phenomenon is that successful service delivery (i.e. recovery of the situation) leads to improved trust as customers feel more confident about the brand. Whether such a paradox exists in real life has been a topic of research since the original claim was made. The research findings are conflicting and inconclusive. In other words, researchers had to stretch the data to come up with the existence of such a paradox in rare cases and restrictive settings. For instance, some researchers concluded that such a paradox exists only if customers perceive the failure to be inconsequential and out of the control zone of the business. I am not sure whether there exists a business which is ready to gamble on that perception in order to benefit from the paradox. Moreover, there is a widespread agreement on the fact that even if the paradox works for the first failure, it definitely doesn't work for the second.

In my own experience, the service recovery paradox is a trivial concept for any care practitioner. It is both unconvincing and irrelevant. If it truly existed, the optimal strategy for any business would be to design their products in a way such that they fail once so that every customer will experience service recovery. Does that make sense? To me, it doesn't. Moreover, I have come across brands with substantial gaps in their service satisfaction and product advocacy ratings. That is to say, their customers are happy with the service they receive, but they are not willing to promote the brand - presumably, because of factors like product performance, quality or price. I will reiterate my take on this: the best way to solve a care issue is to prevent the issue from happening in the first place. If the issue is not avoidable, then the issue handling should, at least, not be unpleasant for the customer. That is to say, issues should be addressed with minimal customer effort.

Minimize the customer effort in issue resolution

Think of a customer calling the helpdesk of a consumer electronics company and writing endless e-mails over and over again to fix his broken smartphone. He explains the same problem to multiple representatives and is transferred from one representative to another, or worse, from one channel to another. Ultimately, he consistently receives the same feedback: "we took note of the case and we will get back to you shortly." But thereafter, it is a black hole: no one ever gets back to him to inform him of a resolution. Think of how annoying that would be. Sometimes, the customer becomes so annoyed that he tries to take revenge by being annoying: sending the same complaint through different channels tens of times or using overly aggressive language. The event turns into a game of "who can be more annoying." In these cases, the company loses no matter what the outcome. It either loses the customer or is forced to find a costly solution to retain a half-happy customer.

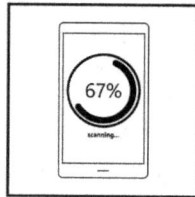   

The one with the self-healing device

Think of the same customer in a near future when the Internet of Things (IoT) has revolutionized issue-handling. With the interconnection of electronic devices, which allows the transfer of data from one device to another, a self-healing device will no longer be an impossible dream. Take the example of an app on the customer's smartphone, which continuously screens the device for technical issues. Such an app can identify the issue even before the customer can, especially if it relates to software or detectable hardware issues. It can run an automatic diagnosis and trigger relevant resolutions (such as filing a service request) on its own without disturbing the customer, or advise the customer proactively which steps need to be taken. Compare the two cases: an endless quarrel with the helpdesk versus an issue being resolved even without the customer realizing there was a problem. Which one requires less customer effort? Which is a more pleasant experience for the customer? Which represents a better care practice?

Customers differ, but similarities exist

Every customer is unique and therefore every customer issue is unique. Having said that, in order to structure the issue-handling processes, we can categorize the type of customers into ten groups based on three criteria: communication style, legitimacy of the issue and willingness to settle. The way you handle these ten customer groups will require different strategies. In the following table, you will find the mapping of the ten distinct customer categories, which will be discussed individually below. It is important that this categorization is incorporated into the training of customer-facing personnel.

Table 4. Categorization of Customers for Issue Handling Purposes

	Communication style			Issue legitimacy		Willingness to settle	
	Silent	Active	Aggressive	Yes	No	High	Low
Genuine muted	√			√		N/A*	
Unoriented	√				√		
Genuine calm		√		√			
Fed up		√		√			√
Chancer		√			√	√	
Whiner		√			√		√
Genuine excitable			√	√		√	
Avenger			√	√			√
Opportunist			√		√	√	
Problem maker			√		√		√

*N/A: It is impossible to settle when you don't even know there is an issue.

These ten groups don't carry an equal weight among customers. In my own experience, "genuine muted" makes up the largest group, followed by "genuine calm" and "unoriented." The other two groups of significant size are "genuine excitable" and "fed up." These five groups make up more than 95% of customers with issues. Despite being small in proportion, the remaining five groups require special handling procedures.

Genuine muted	Genuine calm	Genuine excitable	Fed up	Avenger
Unoriented	Whiner	Chancer	Opportunist	Problem maker

"Genuine muted" is the silent majority

First, it is important to keep in mind that a small fraction of customers complain: the "genuine muted" is actually the silent majority, who do not voice their complaints. There is a wide range of figures available in literature; however, irrespective of what the exact ratio is, it is fair to assume that for every customer who is complaining, there is a handful out there with unvoiced issues. They don't voice them because:

- they don't see the value in the process: they are not sure whether it is worth the time and effort, not sure what they could achieve, not sure whether the issue will be taken seriously and handled properly

- they don't know the process: they are not sure where, when or how to reach out

- they are not complaining types: they don't complain under any circumstances or they don't care to complain

The silent majority poses the largest risk for companies: this is the group of customers that you may lose without even having a chance to try and win back. In that sense, complaining customers are better for business; at least they give you a chance to make things right. I come across companies which obscure their contact information, especially their phone number, on their websites or print materials; they hide it for the sake of controlling service costs. This is an excellent display of a short-sighted management approach: saving a quantifiable amount from service costs (i.e. 20% reduction in contact volume) at the expense of losing an unquantifiable (but much larger) amount due to customer churn. Issues do not go away by not talking about them. Actually, these issues get worse over time. Therefore, the following two objectives should be optimized concurrently:

(1) Minimize the number of customer complaints through elimination of failures.

(2) Maximize the probability of customer reach-out by making it easier to complain. Communicating "contact us" wherever possible (call for action), displaying the contact information visibly, offering multiple contact channels, enabling easy contact (such as click-to-call or click-to-chat) and callback options are all potential facilitators for increased reach out.

Offering more channels to make it easier for a customer to raise an issue comes with the associated burden of integration. Not all channels are equipped to resolve every issue. Although not preferable, escalation is unavoidable in some cases. Nevertheless, escalation rules from one channel to another should be clear for issue handling and tracking. Channels should be connected with each other in a seamless manner. Lack of connectivity between the channels (channel gaps) ruptures the experience and causes extra customer frustration. It is critical to maintain the context and interaction history while shifting between channels. Customer data should be available at each touchpoint in an attempt to avoid customers having to re-explain their issues each time. Interaction history should be recorded properly and in sufficient detail.

"Unoriented customers" is a reality check for your designed customer journey

"Unoriented" represents the group of customers who genuinely believe that they have an issue but their issue is actually a lack of knowledge. For instance, unoriented customers aren't able to enjoy the full benefits of the product because they don't know all the features and how to use them. These customers are typically first-time users for whom the use of your product is not that intuitive. Intuitiveness is not necessarily an objective norm: built-in expectations (which may vary from one person to another) determine whether something is intuitive or not. Expectations are built by the incumbent products used by the customers. Accordingly, it is more likely to observe lack of orientation among customers who have recently switched to your product from a competing product. These customers tend to constantly compare the performance of your product against the products they previously used and have the tendency to get disappointed rather quickly each time they face a difficulty with your product. As the disappointments build up, so does the unvoiced frustration: eventually, they may relapse back to the product they were using previously (the best evil is the one you know). Their difficulties could easily be addressed by simple explanations and tutorials; however, as they do not voice their concerns, they become the group of customers that you lose seemingly for no reason – except for lack of proper onboarding communication.

"Genuine calm" is the signature customer of the
"I have an issue" episode

"Genuine calm" customers are facing a real issue and their sole aim is to solve this issue quietly and quickly. They want to move on. They are the ideal customer type for any business which has failed to prevent an issue from happening. The most important objective in issue handling is to ensure that customers are able to get their issues addressed with minimal effort from the moment of issue occurrence up until its resolution. Some researchers even claim that the level of effort is the best predictive measure for retention and repurchase. Based on my personal experience, I can confirm that the level of effort appears to play the key role in successfully addressing the issues of "genuine calm" customers. Logic says that level of effort should therefore have some impact in the retention of these customers. However, a broader claim (i.e. extrapolation to all customers) would be an exaggeration considering that a large proportion of customers don't even voice out their issues. We will further discuss this topic in more depth in a later chapter.

Customer effort is highly dependent on the ability to resolve issues during the first contact. If you aren't able to resolve the issue immediately, solutions should be developed to minimize additional customer effort. For instance, I use my mobile operator's app to purchase data packages when I am abroad in order to avoid excessive roaming charges. Once, I couldn't complete the purchase as the app kept failing to respond when I submitted the request. I called their helpdesk. The agent on the phone couldn't help me either as they were experiencing system issues. Actually, both the mobile app and the agent were using the same back-end infrastructure, meaning that if I couldn't make the purchase through the mobile app, she couldn't execute an order-on-behalf either. As a result, my issue wasn't solved at the first contact. However, the agent told me that she would set an automatic alert in the system and I would receive a message as soon as the system was up and running. Within half an hour, I received a message and subsequently bought the data package through the app with a few clicks. That message eliminated the need for me to continuously check the availability of the system through the app. It saved the day and turned an otherwise disastrous service experience into something acceptable. I don't know when the mobile operator put this workaround in place; presumably, the first time they faced a similar issue. If so, the very first customer with a genuine issue helped them to improve the experience for other customers.

"Genuine excitable" requires attention beyond
quick issue resolution

The difference between "genuine calm" and "genuine excitable" is the style of expression and tonality. There are few possible drivers for this difference: maybe it is not first time that the customer has experienced an issue with your product and therefore she is losing her patience, or maybe the customer's normal way of expressing herself is more heightened than others, or maybe she is just having a bad day. Quick issue resolution is not necessarily the immediate objective in this case. Above all, we should attempt to calm these customers down by allowing them to vent: (1) Listen to them patiently, (2) Assure them that they are heard and understood, (3) Acknowledge the issue, (4) Apologize if/as necessary. These can be long interactions; I have come across excitable customers who complained nonstop for close to an hour.

"Fed ups" let accumulated frustration out

"Fed up" is a group of customers that we need to work hard to retain. They have a legitimate issue, but they aren't willing to reconcile (i.e. come back to good terms). This is usually the group of customers who have experienced repeated failures with the product and/or services. At the first or second failure, presumably they were a part of the "genuine calm" group. Our consistency in failing likely downgraded them to the "fed up" group. We will discuss how to deal with frustrated customers later in Episode VI.

"Avenger" wants to let off steam more than anything else

"Avenger" represents a group of customers with whom we face an even more strained interaction than the "fed ups." These customers typically use an aggressive communication style as a means to penalize the people who made them upset. They are not necessarily interested in having their issue resolved, as they are not likely to continue using the product. I am sure you have heard or said something along these lines more than once in your life: "I called them and gave them a piece of my mind. And it was ugly." This is usually an impulse reaction of a customer who is annoyed and wants to make the responsible party pay for it. It is highly likely that the store assistant or contact center agent being yelled at is not the person who made this customer angry. Nevertheless, at that moment, whoever represents the company is the antagonist.

"Chancers" and "Opportunists" could offer you a win-win

"Chancer" and "opportunist" are two groups with similar motivation, but different styles. They are usually interested in courtesy gifts, free of charge services or discount offers. Many companies have rigid policies that do not allow their personnel to offer any goodies if there are no valid reasons for doing so. Sometimes, this could be a lost opportunity. Think about these customers as entrepreneurs who are ready to make a win-win deal with you. Offer them something that both parties could benefit from. For instance, offer an incentive motivating them to buy a product you'd like to promote or shop through a channel you'd like to strengthen. Offer them a discount coupon for their next online purchase if promoting your webstore is one of your business objectives. The best way to handle these cases is to quickly distance yourself from discussing any "issues" (as both parties pretty much know that there isn't a genuine issue in place) and wrap up the conversation with kind words: "Thank you for reaching out to us. Our customers are important to us and we appreciate any opportunity to talk to them. I'd like to offer you a discount coupon as a small gift of appreciation."

With some customers, it is all about damage control

"Whiners," "avengers" and "problem makers" are the most difficult customers as they have low willingness to settle the issue, with the added complexity of an aggressive communication style in the case of the latter two groups. Something good will rarely come out of an interaction with a customer who is in a nonconciliatory mood. Thereby, the interaction should be more about damage control than anything else. Staying calm and trying to calm down the customer is the only reasonable way to deal with this type of customer. Any action, verbal or physical cue that may further the customer's anger should be avoided at all costs. The key is not to take the interaction personally and to keep professionalism at all times. Handling difficult customers requires special skills and not all your personnel will possess these skills. It is advisable to set up a "special situation management team" (SSMT) – a team of specifically trained personnel – to handle the most challenging cases. As often as possible, difficult cases should be directed to this team and the situation should be handled in private so that other customers don't have to witness an unpleasant interaction.

It is important to note that redirecting is becoming an increasingly challenging task with the widespread use of social media as a venting channel by angry customers. In that sense, social media is a failure channel for issue handling: once a social media post is out and visible to the network of the posting customer, the damage is done. The issue becomes public and thereafter, damage control is even more difficult. Instead of digging ourselves out of a hole, we should rather target to identify angry customers and handle their complaints before they start broadcasting them on social media. Another public place where you may face difficult customers is the retail store environment. It is unpleasant and uncomfortable for other customers to be forced to observe a heated discussion. This basically ruins the joy of shopping. Especially if the complaint does not directly concern that specific retail point, it is advisable to immediately move the conversation to a private area.

A typical redirection speech may look something like this:

"You are voicing an important issue. Thank you very much for bringing it to our attention. Please be assured that your issue will be taken seriously and handed properly. If you would agree,

I will put you in contact with our expert team in order to develop a solution and address your concerns in full."

Noting that "whiners" and "problem makers" have no legitimate issue, they usually complain for the sake of complaining. It is, of course, impossible to resolve an issue that doesn't actually exist. Therefore, helping these customers is about the issue-handling process (the path), more than the resolution (the destination). Keep calm, listen carefully and repeat the issue in the customer's own language. It is important to make sure that you understand and take the issue seriously even if there is not a real issue in place. Repeat this cycle a few times until the words lose their meaning: until the customer is fully satisfied with the depth and breadth of the complaining he has done. Although unusual, patiently listening and showing compassion regarding a nonissue is a way to fulfill your customer's needs in this case. Don't forget that there are some people out there who nobody listens to, and they expect you to listen to them in exchange for the favor they have done for you by buying your product.

Dealing with "avengers" is no different with the exception that they have a legitimate issue. Therefore, this implies a two-step process: the first step is the same as the one described above, meaning compassionate listening. If you are successful, the "avenger" will transform into a "genuine excitable" or "fed up" customer at the end of the first step, as his need to complain has been satisfied. Thereafter, the focus of the handling process should be transformed into issue resolution.

"The customer is always right," or is he really?

My final remarks relate to the famous "customer is always right" statement. I believe that the "customer is rarely wrong" or "customers always have the right to service" are more appropriate ways to express the phenomenon. The human-minded care concept, defined as "humans taking care of humans," seeks balance between the two sides – which are both humans. Assigning absolute right to be right to the customers may only cause bitterness among your employees. Bitter humans cannot take care of other humans well. Tolerating the difficult customers beyond what is reasonable (as explained above) and offering them better conditions and treatment (for the sake of reconciling) is a betrayal to other customers. Moreover, I have never heard of a brand which values abusive behavior. Staying true to your brand values requires not incentivizing such behavior. No business will ever face more than a handful of these customers; however, when the relationship is damaged beyond repair, the impossible customers should be counseled out in a calm and professional manner. When the relationship reaches a point of beyond possible, it is no longer a question of care; I would let the lawyers draft the terms and language of the counseling out process.

Episode IV – revisited: My client has an issue

A new kind of episode is developing in the world: "my client has an issue." Businesses are emerging to follow up customers' complaints and needed service by validating customer rights and claiming compensation on their behalf for various issues they have encountered. This trend is moving the issue handling-process from a business-to-consumer setting to a business-to-business (i.e. two businesses dealing with each other) setting while equalizing the playing field in terms of knowledge and resources. Probably the most well-known example in this area is AirHelp, which helps airline customers recoup compensation for delayed, cancelled or overbooked flights in exchange for a success fee (reported to be 25% of the compensation). Through the AirHelp website and mobile app, airline customers can initiate a claim by filling out a form that provides the details of their disrupted flights within the last three years. AirHelp states that less than 2% of worldwide airline customers, eligible for compensation, understand their entitlements even though the eligibility and rights are defined in detail in many jurisdictions. In addition to the limited understanding of their rights, many customers don't have the expertise, time or will to follow up the claims process on their own. AirHelp states that they have assisted more than 10 million passengers since they went live in 2013, although they have not shared any concrete data regarding the percentage of claims resulting in compensation.

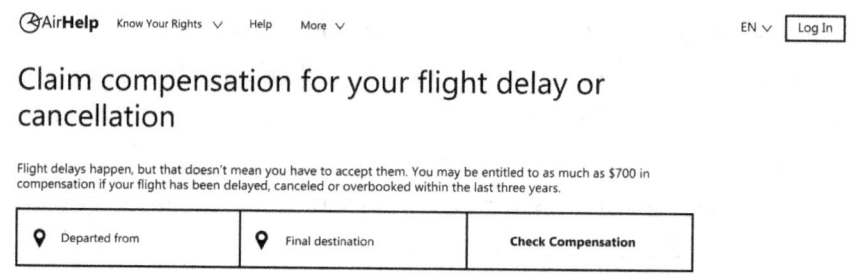

Not all issues are suitable for outsourcing: a sufficient amount of monetary outcome must be at stake. However, the emergence of AI-supported bots, which handle claims on behalf of customers, will reduce the threshold. It is likely that we will eventually end up with a scenario where the bots of both parties, customer and business, will negotiate with each other to reach a settlement. All in all, I think the complaint outsourcing trend will increase the pressure on businesses to be more transparent in terms of customer rights and more proactive in terms of issue-handling. This conclusion supports the principles we have highlighted in the previous sections.

Episode V: I have a suggestion

A suggestion is an open-ended recommendation received from a customer regarding any aspect of your business. Suggestions differ from surveys in two ways: (1) surveys are prompted whereas suggestions may or may not be prompted, (2) surveys are designed and have a standard set of questions whereas suggestions are freestyle text or conversation on any topic. Accordingly, surveys have defined boundaries, whereas the scope of suggestions is unlimited – or at least limited by the imagination of the person making the suggestion. Moreover, survey results are usually treated collectively whereas suggestions need to be treated one by one. In that regard, suggestions are a lot like customer complaints but they don't necessarily contain any expression of dissatisfaction.

A suggestion is a very valuable piece of information because of its spontaneous nature. Don't be afraid to seek suggestions from your customers through one simple, open-ended question: "How can we do better?" or "What can we improve?" Only a small group of customers actually makes suggestions.

This does not mean that their suggestions are not relevant to a large group of customers. A suggestion is usually the result of a specific observation and identifies an area of potential improvement. For each suggestion made by a customer, it is fair to assume that there are a handful more customers out there with similar observations. However, those customers probably did not want to go through the effort of writing a suggestion. Accordingly, suggestions should be taken seriously as they can provide unique insights that could not be achieved by any other source of customer feedback.

Suggestions should be meticulously followed up

Suggestions may come with a name or may be made anonymously. As a business, we should encourage customers to leave their names when making suggestions as this allows further engagement. This encouragement could be as simple as putting a clear note on the physical or digital suggestion form: "Please leave us your e-mail address or phone number. We are looking forward to reaching out to you to better understand your suggestion and inform you about the actions taken following your suggestion." Thereafter, the suggestion should be followed up in the same manner as customer-complaint handling. Contact the customer to thank them for their suggestion and update them on any steps taken following their suggestion. The more concrete and detailed the steps taken by the company, the greater the customer satisfaction will be. Nevertheless, a simple confirmation that their suggestion was shared with the relevant development or execution team is usually pleasing enough. We should also encourage the customer to make suggestions again in the future and offer him a symbolic gift of appreciation for making the effort to leave a suggestion. A small discount on the next purchase or points in the loyalty program are typical perks used in practice. Suggestions usually come from your most progressive customers, who possess a critical mind and creative thinking aptitude. It is vital to make these customers feel that their suggestions have been taken seriously and their ideas are valued. This is a great opportunity for a company to strengthen its relationship with its forward-thinking customers.

Suggestions may lead to innovative improvements

Receiving suggestions should be a goal of every company. Suggestions lead to business improvements, which may have otherwise not been considered, while presenting opportunities to bond with your customers. Facilitating suggestion submission could be as simple as featuring suggestion links somewhere visible on your website or putting suggestion boxes near the cashiers in a retail environment. As a caring business, don't forget to have paper forms and pens available next to the physical suggestion boxes.

One great example of a suggestion box application is one offered by Nordstrom. They use the UserVoice platform (https://nordstrom.uservoice.com) to allow their customers to share ideas or suggestions and to vote for an existing comment. The Nordstrom team replies directly to customer comments and the ongoing communication is made visible and transparent to everyone.

Episode VI: I am frustrated

Goods fail, services fail. This is a fact of life. Customers acknowledge the possibility of failures and generally tolerate them. They are disappointed with failures, but they don't necessarily consider abandoning your product because of a single failure. Repeated failures, on the other hand, cause frustration. When a product fails, services come into play. If the service fails to address the product failure, then this is a double failure. Depending on the customer's tolerance limit, a double failure could cause a level of frustration sufficient enough to make the customer want to stop using the product. More tolerant customers could still stay longer to experience the third, fourth and subsequent failures, but everyone has a breaking point. The amount of tolerance a customer would display towards your failures depends on the credibility you have built as a business up to that moment. Think about a failure as a shock in your relationship with the customer and your credibility as a cushion absorbing the shock.

Reconciliation is an attempt to save the relationship

In any case, it is critical to reconcile with frustrated customers. Reconciliation is about identifying customers with negative product sentiments and changing these sentiments by carefully listening to them and resolving the customer's issues. There are three broad ways to identify frustrated customers:

(1) *Self-declaration:* customers voicing their frustration spontaneously

(2) *Surveys:* customers voicing their frustration when asked

(3) *Sentiment reading:* service personnel or an AI-powered solution rating a customer's sentiment

Having said that, instead of waiting for the frustration to be voiced or spotted on an occasional basis, the most effective way is to identify it proactively, based on customers' behavior. Symptoms of frustration and warning signs of potential churn are usually visible for companies reading the chain of events carefully with that perspective in mind. Here is a personal story: most of us have client relationships with multiple banks. One for daily transactions, to pay the bills and credit cards. Maybe one for the mortgage and another for savings and investment.

Maybe a dormant one that you barely use. I am personally a client of four banks – actually, I was a client of four banks. I was not particularly happy with one of my banks: their online banking was substandard and their charges were high. Each time I used their online banking services, they asked to me complete a satisfaction survey. Each time, I did it, marking them very low. I was tied to the bank due to some temporarily illiquid assets, but I managed to sell some of the assets and put in an order to transfer a portion of the available funds to an account in another bank. A day after the transfer order, I received a call from the bank. The agent on the phone was trying to validate the transfer order for security reasons. I confirmed the order and she confirmed that it had been executed earlier that morning. Interesting! Why did not they bother confirming the order before executing it? Wasn't it a bit too late? Anyway, that is not the essence of the story.

A few months later, I managed to sell some more of the assets that were being held in that bank and transferred the cash balance out. They called me again to validate the order. We repeated this ritual two more times and, in less than a year, I had a zero-balance left in that account. During their last call to validate the transfer order, I asked them how I could close my account. They told me to call the service helpline. Who was I talking to up to that moment? I am no longer a customer of that bank, but the most interesting part of the story is that I talked with the bank's representatives four times during that period and none of them ever cared to ask why I was transferring out my money out of my account at their bank. They validated the orders against the potential risk of fraud and executed them quickly. They were kind on the phone. But, overall, they provided disastrous care: they didn't even care that they were witnessing a profitable customer churning out. They definitely had no predictive capabilities either, even in the presence of every possible indicator of imminent churn.

Businesses should be vigilant against these indicators whenever they make an important business intervention, such as changing a policy or discontinuing a product offer. Moreover, competitive moves run the risk of fueling frustration. Factors which previously never bothered customers could become sources of frustration later when the competition introduces offers that are more appealing.

Reconciliation requires special skills

Reconciliation interactions are critical and should be executed only by the most skilled and experienced service personnel. Companies that select and train the right personnel for this purpose are better positioned to get strong results, provided that they are also ready to trust their personnel and empower them in the right manner. One type of empowerment is letting your service personnel handle customer issues in any way they deem appropriate up to a predefined budget limit. This can increase their business ownership and motivate them to find more creative and personalized solutions. This approach should only be used when the underlying drivers of customer frustration is versatile or not very well-known and only the most experienced service personnel should be employed in the process.

Alternatively, a more structured approach could streamline the process and help service personnel deliver consistently good results. Rules of empowerment should be clearly defined, including the underlying cause of frustration and a pre-defined remedy for each driver. The remedy could be explanatory or compensatory. In many cases, just reaching out to the frustrated customer and listening carefully can eliminate the frustration. Humans appreciate it when they are taken seriously and they relax when they are able to get the frustration off their chest. Customers should feel that someone is clearly accountable for what caused them to get frustrated in the first place. They should feel that their frustration is not going unheard or being treated with indifference.

Reconciliation remedies should address the source of frustration

The remedy offered to the customers should be relevant to the cause of their frustration. Otherwise, it could further fuel their anger. For instance, if customers are frustrated with the product performance due to a perceived discrepancy between the advertised and actual delivery, offering to replace their product with an identical unit – which is likely to deliver the same performance – would only result in an eventual customer outburst. Here, it makes sense to refer back to the failure categories that we discussed in Episode IV and map the underlying causes of frustration into one of the following categories:

Table 5. Remedies to Handle Frustration

Failure Category	Underlying Cause - Example	Remedy - Example
Core functionality – Goods	Product repeatedly broken (due to a design or manufacturing flaw)	• Express your apology • Offer refund or replacement with a different product version • Inform the customer that the case will be escalated to the product development and/or manufacturing teams
Core functionality – Service	Product not delivered	• Check the product delivery status and unblock/expedite the delivery • Express your apology • Offer a free (express) shipment option for the next purchase

Services	Waiting on the line for half an hour to reach a service agent	◆ Express your apology and, if relevant, explain why lines are overloaded ◆ Explain the other service options (e.g. self-service) and less busy channels (e.g. live chat) ◆ Inform the customer about call-back options, if available ◆ Inform the customer about the typical peak and low volume hours
Communication	Purchased the product on the promise that the offer represents the lowest price available on the market. Later discovered a lower price offer	◆ Check and validate the customer claim (preferably on a real time basis) ◆ Express your apology ◆ Offer to reimburse the price difference and include a small gift (such as an additional discount coupon) as a form of compensation

Channel and touchpoint	Treated impolitely at retail	• Carefully note the details of the event and explain to the customer that the case will be investigated ♦ Investigate the case and, if required, ask the responsible manager to call the customer and apologize while explaining the internal actions taken (without excessive details)

We have now completed the review of the six care episodes. These episodes are designed according to the care principles outlined in the previous chapter. These episodes make up the core of the care processes for every business. However, it is natural to have some variations from one business to another. We also need to keep in mind that the care principles should be applied in everything we do as a business – not only in these six processes. Moreover, we noted that preventing issues from happening should be the overarching goal for any business. In line with this goal, I will conclude this section by introducing the concept of preventive and predictive care.

Preventive and predictive care

In this section, we will borrow some concepts from the machinery and equipment industry to build a relevant application for customer care. Humans deserve more care than machinery and equipment. It would be shameful to not offer them at least this level of care.

There are three types of maintenance applied to equipment:

(1) *Reactive (breakdown) maintenance:* Repairing equipment that is already broken with the aim of bringing it back to operational mode

(2) *Preventive maintenance:* Maintenance performed regularly while the equipment is still operational in order to reduce the risk of failures

(3) *Predictive maintenance:* Predicting the occurrence of failure in advance and performing maintenance to avoid it.

Humans deserve no less care than machines

Predictive maintenance is the optimal option as it reduces the risk of unplanned break downs while incurring less cost than the successive, periodical maintenance activities. However, the effectiveness of predictive maintenance depends on the ability of predicting failures.

Based on this analogy, we can define preventive care as bombarding customers with all possible information that could help them avoid potential issues. On the other hand, predictive care is applying predictive analytics to discover use cases where customer issues can proactively be resolved or avoided.

Let's go back to the mobile operator example. Many people travel abroad during the summer months to enjoy the sun and the beach. It is not that difficult to predict a common question: what are the communication costs (roaming charges) abroad? One option for finding the answer is calling your mobile phone operator's helpdesk to ask. However, many mobile operators take a preventive approach to this issue by communicating summer tips to their mailing list in the early days of the season. They include pointers on how to avoid excessive calling, messaging and data usage costs while traveling abroad. They also remind customers how to reach their service helpdesk when they are in another country. "Don't leave your phone under the sun for prolonged periods" is a trivial warning that is usually featured in some of these communications. Obviously, everyone on the mailing list, regardless of whether they are going abroad for vacation or not, receives this communication: it is preventive, but not predictive.

Actually, as soon as you enter the roaming zone, your mobile operator recognizes the connection through a foreign network. Some mobile operators send you a short message with the rate card (for incoming and outgoing calls, text messages and mobile data use). This is a good practice of predictive care: providing whatever the customer needs at the right time and the right place. Operators with excellent selling skills will even take it to the next level: they warn their customers about the inhibitive roaming costs and advise them to buy prepaid packages to avoid excessive costs. This is a good practice of sales through care. Some operators take it further by including in their communication the emergency numbers in the foreign country. This is a good example of the "we are always watching your back" approach.

Avoiding the next issue should be the ultimate goal

One of the best occasions to practice predictive care is when resolving the current issue. In literature, this approach is sometimes referred as "next issue avoidance." In many cases, there is a strong correlation between the issue being experienced by a customer and potential issues he may experience over time. Correlation analysis between the different issue types or the issue types and customer profiles could reveal hidden relationships and lead to actionable insights. The correlation is usually driven by the recurrence of the original issue or the characteristics of a given customer profile (for instance, difficulties resulting from the customer's lack of technological savvy). It is wise to try to avoid future issues as soon as the current issue is addressed. This can be achieved either through on-the-spot communication or sending a follow-up communication (via e-mail), depending on the nature of communication required to address the downstream issues. Successful implementation is dependent on a radical change in mindset: shifting the focus from cost management (i.e. minimizing the issue-handling duration) to improving the customer experience through education (i.e. minimizing the average number of issues faced by the customer). This change should start with training and motivating the service squad (i.e. the whole company) to anticipate and forwardly resolve the downstream customer issues.

As we have seen, the principles of care accompany every stage of the customer lifecycle and have lasting effects on whether a customer remains interested in a given brand or not. Consistently exercising care at the right time and through the right channel is a sign of a care-first business. However, being a company that genuinely cares for its customers and actually having the ability to offer that care are two separate matters. It is now time to turn our attention to what it takes to be a care-first business from a capability standpoint.

CHAPTER 6

Care Channels

U p to this moment, we have mainly discussed principles, policies and processes. A capable infrastructure is another core enabling element of human-minded care. Even with every good intention in place, no business can excel in care without the ability to reach out to their customers and enable their customers to reach out to them easily across a multitude of channels.

In its broadest definition, care infrastructure is composed of any interaction point in which the customer is exposed to the brand as care should be a defining element in everything we do. Above-the-line channels (such as TV, cinema, radio, print/digital media and outdoor advertising) and certain below-the-line channels (such as events and sponsorships) are mainly used to increase brand awareness and sales. Although these channels are not covered in this chapter, the activities taking place in these channels should strictly follow the care principles discussed in Chapter II.

We defined the right channel as the one with which the customer feels the most comfortable for a specific interaction. This definition encompasses two variables: customer profile and interaction type. We will first categorize the care channels into broad groups to define the characteristics of customer interactions and the factors determining their success in provoking engagement for different customer profiles. This categorization will also help us to highlight the differences among the channels in terms of service cost, quality and scalability.

We can broadly categorize the care channels into two types, depending on who delivers the service:

(1) *"I will help myself"*: self-service

(2) *"I want someone to help me"*: human-assisted service

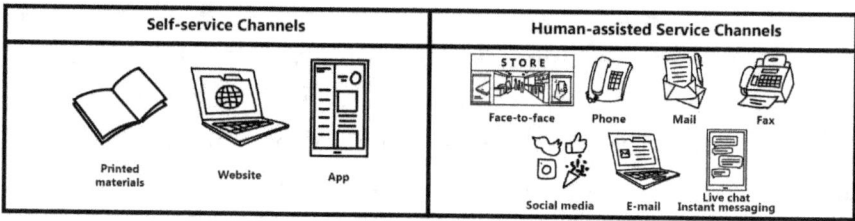

Self-service is a godsend for businesses as it improves customer satisfaction and reduces service costs at the same time. Moreover, these channels are fully scalable as the service activity is outsourced to the person in need of the service. In other words, the customer herself is the service agent and there are as many service agents as there are customers. You may also define self-service as a way to empower customers to solve their own problems, eliminating the need to consult anyone. That empowerment alone, being self-sufficient, is a source of incremental happiness for humans. Thereby, enlarging the boundaries of self-service should be a core strategy for every business. This enlargement involves two building blocks:

1. Increasing self-service options: it is important to explore which customer interactions are suitable for self-service, especially in light of technological advancements. Self-service is increasingly based on digital solutions, a topic we will later discuss at length. In line with the increasing proportion of digital natives among us, possibil-

ities are flourishing to equip the whole customer journey with self-service solutions. The critical success factor is to ensure that customers can resolve their issues on their own without going through too much hassle. That is to say, it is essential to make multiple easy-to-access, easy-to-use self-service options available.

2. Increasing the popularity of self-service among customers: making human-assisted channels less accessible in order to force customers to self-service is a commonly applied trick in the industry. It is effective, but not sustainable as it is likely to result in lower customer satisfaction. The viable way to improve the popularity of self-service solutions is to increase awareness of their existence among customers and to incentivize their use. Incentives could be indirect, such as lower implied effort for the customer or improved accessibility to service (i.e. anytime, anywhere). They could also be direct, such as reduced service costs or loyalty program points. As an example, many banks charge a fee (around $20) to block a credit card by calling their contact center whereas blocking the credit card through online banking is usually free of charge. Introducing a service surcharge for the human-assisted channel (or reducing/eliminating the service surcharge for the self-service channel) is a frequently used direct incentive.

Despite the increasing importance of self-service, human intervention will always be necessary. Certain cases are still better-handled through human-to-human interaction. We will take a look at this in more detail in the final chapter of the book. All being said, self- and assisted-services are now being revolutionized by the emergence and propagation of Virtual Customer Assistants (VCAs) – frequently called digital robots, chatbots, voice bots or simply bots. VCAs are designed to simulate conversations that can deliver information and act on behalf of a customer to perform transactions. VCAs usually consist of:

- User interfaces to receive requests and deliver responses via speech or text

- Search engines and knowledge bases

- Natural language processing (NPL) capability to understand the spoken language and respond in a natural tone

- Context analysis capability to analyze intent and provide customized responses or actions.

Service landscape revolutionized by the AI solutions

VCAs can be implemented on websites and apps to convert these self-service channels to bot-assisted channels. For instance, instead of a customer searching for answers through the FAQs, a VCA can pull out the relevant answer from the knowledge base and share it with the customer. Alternatively, if a customer spends more than a minute or two in the FAQ section of a website, a live chat could pop up asking the customer whether she needs help or not. Live chat could be handled by the VCA unless the topic requires escalation to a human agent. It is important to keep in mind that if a customer can't succeed with self-service options, he will pick up the phone to seek assistance. The time lost exploring the self-service options is likely to result in customer frustration. You would frequently hear your customer saying, "I should have just called in the first place."

Alternatively, VCAs could fully replace human agents in certain tasks, and support them in others, while interacting with the customers in human-assisted channels. Actually, we observe that VCAs are increasingly playing the gatekeeper role – handling simple, repetitive requests and deciding on what and when to direct to human agents.

VCAs offer certain advantages over their human counterparts. They are always available (24/7) and follow the built-in procedures consistently. They create a full audit trial, work at machine speed and pose almost no operational risk. Moreover, the underlying technology allows easy scale up and down in the face of service demand variability. In parallel to the advancements in technology, VCAs are becoming more proficient in understanding the context and subtle differences in everyday language. They are increasingly able to engage in more human-like conversations from initiation of an interaction to successful completion of a task. The capability of VCA assistance in live conversations, such as chat and instant messages, is proven. Presumably, further enhancements are required to properly handle exchanges when context analysis and progressive learning are not possible. This concerns cases in which the whole content is provided at once, such as reading, fully understanding and replying to written text.

Traditional versus Digital Channels

We can also categorize the channels as traditional or digital based on their historical use and the extent in which their use has been accepted by all customer groups.

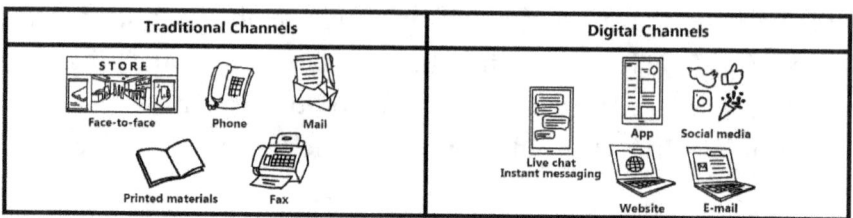

It is important to note that boundaries between the traditional and digital channels are becoming blurred as channels become increasingly integrated. Think about a chatbot that pops up for assistance when the customer is shopping on your website. It is designed to answer simple inquiries and facilitate purchase. This is a digital solution in a digital channel enabling assisted service. Take the same digital solution and place it in your store. For instance, you can place a touch screen that allows customers to access your website and interact with the chatbot – or better yet, you could design an even more engaging user interface (with a level of gamification) for use in your stores. This is a digital solution in a traditional channel enabling assisted service. When customers visit your store, they will have two choices for receiving help: they can speak with a store assistant or use the touch screen solution. This increasing integration of channels allows customers to freely choose among different interaction options and switch from one interaction to another on the go.

Significant variances are observed across the different customer profiles in terms of adapting the traditional and digital channels. Digital native customers, typically born after 1980s, are – by definition – more inclined to adapt the digital channels.

Moreover, being a natural user of social media and somewhat addicted to instant gratification, their expectations from an interaction differ substantially. For instance, an Instagram enthusiast may prefer visual interactions. On the other hand, older customers still continue to favor the traditional channels, such as F2F and voice interactions – even mail and fax in niche cases. Understanding and segmenting the customer base by developing customer personas could help businesses offer the right mix of channels and allow a smoother flow of interactions along the customer journey.

Due to its public nature and increasing significance, social media is a channel that deserves special attention from every business. We will open up an aside here to discuss its relevance in care interactions.

Social media and messaging apps

I think it is important to treat the messaging apps and social media as two separate channel categories even though the former is sometimes classified under the broader social media channel in other resources. This type of classification could make sense in a different context. However, in the context of customer interaction, messaging apps such as WhatsApp, Facebook Messenger, WeChat and Viber exhibit the characteristics of a live chat channel in terms of the nature of interaction. Thereby, they are not in the same category as other major social media platforms, such as Facebook, Instagram, Twitter or LinkedIn.

Social media is used by businesses primarily for commercial communication. Businesses tend to see the social media interactions as a one-way conversation similar to the above-the-line channels. It is an efficient medium for discovery and connection as a result of the public nature and broad reach of the information exchanged. It is also an ideal channel for proactive care interactions – for instance, to broadcast tips and tricks that would help your customers get the most out of your products or reduce the risk of misuse and eventual product failure.

Social media is a two-way communication channel

However, as a growing trend, customers perceive social media as the fastest way to interact with a business. For them, it is a two-way conversation similar to face-to-face, direct engagement channels (below-the-line channels). Considering the added pressure of public conversations, businesses have no choice but to act. And they need to act fast. Customers contacting the business via e-mail are usually prepared to wait 24 hours for a reply, but social media customers expect a response within the hour.

We can categorize customer interactions into two broad categories: general questions and personal issues. Social media is well-suited for handling general questions: public exchange of such information could help increase awareness on the topic among the other customers who witness the communication. However, it is a less than ideal channel for handling personal issues. Due to the public nature of social media, personal and confidential information (such as account details or discount coupons/codes) must be exchanged somewhere else. Moreover, it is challenging to maintain an all-in-one communication flow (for complicated personal issues) through tweets, comments or posts. It is likely that you will have to change the channel to complete the customer request. As social media platforms are poorly integrated with CRM systems and other communication channels, this transition frequently results in a breakup of the flow of communication and a loss of information.

Personal issues usually come in the form of a complaint. It is never a good idea to have customer complaints publicized. In that sense, social media is a failure channel for complaint-handling: once the complaint is public, the damage is done. Thereafter, it is all about damage control.

Responsiveness (i.e. time between the customer's post and the business' response) becomes the most important factor in such a social media interaction. Unattended posts could go viral and result in a credibility meltdown. Social media has an amplifying effect: one negative interaction could attract an uncalled-for amount of attention from other customers and turn into a PR disaster.

All you want to demonstrate to your customer and, more importantly, to the general public is your responsiveness and your ability to resolve issues quickly. How you achieve this is irrelevant and should better remain undisclosed; other customers should not be exposed to how you handle the chain of events from the original customer post to issue resolution. Therefore, if possible, the discussion should be redirected to a private communication venue. One option is asking the complaining customer to share his contact details via a private message and you reach out to him via phone or e-mail. The dream outcome would be to have the complaining customer make a positive post about the fantastic way you handled their issue.

It is also advisable to separate the social media handle for commercial communications from the care handle. No business wants a mix of glorifying self-published content (such as beautiful photos of your product) and disparaging customer-created content (such as photos of product failures) on the same social media feed. If you have one handle, these two types of content will unavoidably be mixed. Moreover, the negative content will attract more customer attention.

On the other hand, messaging apps are well suited for care interactions due to their private and one-to-one nature. Platforms with end-to-end encryption offer peace of mind to customers in terms of data protection. Messaging apps can be integrated into the CRM systems and other communication channels, allowing a seamless transition between channels. Moreover, their inherent speed and responsiveness are further enhanced by the implementation of chatbots. We will further look into this point in the final chapter. In terms of popularity among customers, the monthly average number of users for messaging apps has already surpassed that of social media. All in all, messaging apps are likely to become a dominant channel for care interactions in the course of the next decade, coming head-to-head with voice.

Messaging apps are the channel which witnesses the highest level of AI deployment for automatic response. Chatbots increasingly manage the first-level support tasks, such as answering FAQs and executing the early stages of the issue-handling process. Many standard solutions are available online to help businesses build a chatbot for Facebook Messenger in less than thirty minutes. These standard solutions are easily customizable by setting AI rules, such as: "if the customer writes something that contains…, bot replies with…" As of 2019, chatbot is a business standard in customer inquiry handling in messaging apps: more than 100,000 chatbots are already operating in Facebook Messenger at the time of writing.

Live, gapping and passive channels

The mode of interaction is another categorization factor with strong implications when engaging with customers. We can count three modes of interaction: live, gapping and passive. "Live" refers to a continuous interaction with responses exchanged in a matter of seconds (or minutes, if the service level is pretty poor). "Gapping" refers to an interaction composed of actions taken at discrete intervals; the responses are therefore usually exchanged in a matter of hours or days. "Passive" refers to the lack of back and forth interactions.

Live Channels	Gapping Channels	Passive Channels
STORE Face-to-face Phone Live chat Instant messaging	Mail Social media Fax	Website App Printed materials

As mentioned before, implementation of VCAs revolution-izes the use of websites and apps by bringing live interaction into these otherwise passive channels. Moreover, mobile apps are turning into a gateway between the customer and the con-tact center, allowing customers to reach out to service agents via "click-to-call," live chat and video call options. It also allows customers to request call-backs and schedule appointments at their preferred time.

We can combine all the categorizations up to now in one ta-ble, which gives a complete picture of the nature of interactions across all channels.

	Traditional Channels				Digital Channels				
	Passive	Gapping	Live		Passive		Gapping		Live
	Print	Mail/fax	Face-to -face	Phone	Website	App	E-mail	Social Media	Chat/Instant Message
Self- service	✓				✓	✓			
Assisted Service		✓	✓	✓			✓	✓	✓

Note: VCA can covert Website and Mobile App into live channels

Based on the table above, we can interpret the trends that are commonly observed in practice:

(1) The popularity of the voice channel can be explained by the fact that it is the only live traditional channel with reach. In the 1960s, the introduction of a helpdesk was a breakthrough innovation. Customers were finally able to access services from home (or wherever they could find a fixed line phone), eliminating the need to visit a branch office. With the emergence and popularization of internet-powered digital solutions, voice has been losing prominence over the last two decades. Having said that, it is still the most dominant support channel, especially for technical issue-handling and for customers above 40.

(2) With the emergence of new live channels, the weight of gapping channels will continue to decline. E-mail is especially in decline due to its irresponsive, slow moving and inefficient nature, coupled with the implied customer effort. Having said that, e-mail will remain a key channel for outbound contacts as it is an efficient one-to-many communication means. It can be automated and person- alized based on customer segmentation. It is inexpen- sive to set up and run; moreover, it is mobile accessible. Therefore, it is particularly useful for outbound cam- paigns (selling, upselling and cross-selling).

(3) Social media is similar in nature to e-mail although it offers customers the benefit of putting public pressure on the business. However, for written communication, live chat is likely to become the dominant channel as it is a live interaction.

(4) In live channels, live chat and instant messaging are gain- ing popularity over voice as they present the possibility of a communication pause. Live chat/IM interferes less with the daily flow of events and allows both the customer and agent to multitask.

Peer-to-peer (P2P)

Up until now, all the channels we have mentioned have been owned and controlled channels. However, in today's connected world, influenced channels have a growing significance and deserve the full attention of any business. Peer-to-peer (P2P) is the most important influenced channel: it is the channel where the "expert" customers help the regular customers find answers to their questions and resolve their issues. Expert customers are usually the outspoken members of forums with hundreds of entries and various forum badges.

If your expert customers are able to help your other customers better than your own service agents, you have a problem. This could mean three things:

(1) You don't fully understand how your products are being used by customers, how they fail and which actions to take when they fail

(2) Your agents are not properly selected, trained or motivated

(3) P2P is more accessible than your support options

Yet you are still lucky to have some "expert" customers who can help others. Maybe you should consider hiring them: as remote service agents, they can pick up customer requests and help your customers virtually.

Final thoughts

Care execution requires people, processes and infrastructure. This infrastructure owns both digital and physical elements. Each service point should act as part of an integrated ecosystem. They should:

- Be connected with each other for an omni-channel service experience. It is important to keep in mind that channel silos affect the customer experience negatively.

- Have access to individual customer history and service status

- Be equipped with service tools and personnel who are fully trained on customer handling procedures and escalation rules

- Be empowered to initiate proactive solutions

- Be automatically guided towards preventive and predictive actions

A common customer information depository, which stores a complete record of every interaction (purchase history, call recordings, e-mail correspondence, loyalty actions, website visits, retail store visits, etc.), is a key asset. It should be owned and managed by the Customer Care team. This requires the synchronization of all the information available in various systems and integration of off-the-system information.

Omnichannel communication platforms provide a holistic view of the customer journey as the customer interaction moves through a variety of channels. This is critical for the continuity of the customer information flow across the channels and helps each channel owner have a better context, resolve the issues quickly and identify the most relevant recommendation for each customer.

One omnichannel challenge is figuring out how to integrate multiple channels in a way that ensures customers don't have to repeat their issue as they move from one channel to another. The notion of being connected all the time increases customer expectations to be able to reach service 24/7. Delivering 24/7 service with human agents is both cost prohibitive and inefficient. Many times, it also means extremely unpleasant scheduling for service agents. Thereby, smart self-service (online communities and step-by-step video tutorials) and automated solutions play a key role in satisfying this customer expectation. All in all, the most fundamental customer expectation is to have their issue resolved quickly and with minimal effort. If the customers can do it by themselves, in their own time and in their own space, without the need to talk to another person, it is likely to be a much better solution for them.

It is wise to ask customers how many channels they use when seeking help, why they feel the need to use more than one channel, and what makes them suffer the most in a multichannel journey. Customers facing difficulties provide invaluable insights that can help businesses eliminate the disconnections between channels and reduce customer effort.

CHAPTER 7

Performance Management

Accoding to the economic theory, individuals, consciously or unconsciously, aim to maximize their welfare. We can define welfare as the individual's own assessment of his or her physical and mental health and happiness. The key question is: how much incremental welfare does a customer derive from your brand given the prices and income? This incremental welfare corresponds to the customer experience, the cumulative outcome of the customer's interactions with every aspect of a brand, and it is the strongest driver of all business metrics and their future progression. For a profit-seeking business, maximizing the bottom-line boils down to optimizing customer welfare and the long-run economic constraints. Aiming for unlimited customer welfare (i.e. a utopic customer experience) is out of the question for any business due to its associated cost. For instance, any business could make customer welfare infinite by not charging for anything (i.e. offering everything for free). However, such a business won't survive in the long term. Instead, businesses try to optimize customer welfare. This is not contradictory to our approach as human-minded care is about defining and delivering what is essential. It is not about delivering unsustainable extravagance.

All business activities – including care – should be managed in a way to maximize its contribution to this collective optimization drive. However, there are two major challenges in this optimization exercise:

1. Defining the relationship between business activities and customer welfare: Customer welfare is a complex, abstract concept which is difficult to quantify. For instance, how much customer welfare improvement would you achieve by shortening the average helpline waiting time by two minutes? By offering a free-of-charge delivery service? By increasing the number of sales assistants in your stores? By extending the warranty duration by three months or warranty scope to cover damaged caused by use? How would all of these compare to the welfare damage caused by increasing the price of your product by 5%? How much more do you need to invest in order to achieve the next increment in customer welfare?

2. Defining the relationship between customer welfare and bottom-line: As discussed in depth, it is widely accepted that higher customer welfare (that is to say, better customer experience) results in improved loyalty (i.e. brand retention or increased share of customer spend) and more positive word-of-mouth (i.e. supporting customer acquisition). However, how much more retention or referrals do you actually achieve by the incremental customer welfare?

In order to explore the answers to these complex questions, we will focus specifically on care activities in the rest of the chapter while noting that our observations and conclusions can easily be extended to any other business area.

Care frequently turns into a cost-optimization exercise

Care costs are easily quantifiable whereas the return from the care investment is almost impossible to quantify. Businesses tend to support spending with predictable return-on-investment. Accordingly, care frequently turns into a cost optimization exercise while ensuring a certain level of customer welfare, which is measured through various customer satisfaction indicators. The sought-after level is usually defined by industry standards and varies significantly from one industry to another. Thus, notoriously, some industries are known for poor service because the industry participants aren't motivated to do better. In other words, there is a gentlemen's agreement between the participants to deliver poor service for the sake of eliminating care-based competition and saving costs. However, this approach isn't sustainable in the long run. Customers compare one care experience to another, regardless of the industry. Waiting on the line for fifteen minutes to reach an agent is a poor service level whether it is the helpdesk of a bank or an airline. As customer expectations are developed progressively by companies that care, industries with notoriously poor service are becoming more and more susceptible to disruption through care.

At this stage, it probably makes sense to recall the Customer Lifetime Value (CLV) equation we defined earlier to establish a cost and benefit relationship for care activities:

$$\text{CLV} = \Sigma_{t=1}^{T} PV[MC_t] + \Sigma_{t=1}^{T} (PV[I_t^+ - I_t^-] - PV[C_t^c]) - C_{\text{acquisition}}$$

MC_t: marginal contribution (earnings; revenue minus the cost of products sold)

I_t^+: value of positive impressions

I_t^-: value of negative impressions

C_t^{ci}: cost of direct customer investment (i.e. loyalty and retention programs, services, incentives)

We defined that care impacts three parameters of this equation: retention duration (T), customer spending (MC_t) and impressions ($I_t^+ - I_t^-$). Focusing only on the cost of care and assuming that no other direct customer investment is made, we can reorganize the CLV equation as follows:

$$\Sigma_{t=1}^{T} PV[C_t^c] = \Sigma_{t=1}^{T} PV[MC_t] + \Sigma_{t=1}^{T} (PV[I_t^+ - I_t^-] - C_{acquisition} - CLV$$

C_t^c: cost of care

Based on our discussion up to this point, we can structure the customer care cost as follows:

C_t^c = Cost of Care Episodes (i.e. Cost of Reactive and Proactive Services) + Cost of care incurred by other functions (as a result of the "care in everything we do" activities)

To help demystify the optimization exercise, let's look at a hypothetical case. Assume that despite increasing our care investment by $1 (present value), we haven't observed any change in our value parameters (i.e. retention duration, customer spending or impressions). As the cost of acquisition is a sunk cost (i.e. nonchanging at a point in time), that $1 investment increase will result in a $1 decrease in the CLV – that is to say, on your business' bottom-line. Theoretically speaking, care investment is optimized at the point where any additional spending would result in a decline in CLV as the value parameters become irresponsive to a further care investment. This means that a saturation point has been reached and the incremental customer welfare generated (if generated at all) by the additional care investment doesn't result in improved loyalty or advocacy.

The plateauing effect, diminishing and eventually disappearing marginal rate of return, is widely accepted in literature for two relationships:

1. Relationship between the care investment and customer satisfaction (as a proxy for customer welfare): Think

about this as the point where you manage to provide everything that is essential to the customer. Anything beyond is trivial or unimportant.

2. Relationship between customer satisfaction and customer loyalty/advocacy: For instance, the number of products a customer can possibly buy (or, the number of people a customer can possibly reach out to) has a natural limit regardless of how satisfied she is.

Thereby, we are facing a double plateauing effect which paves the way to a meaningful optimization exercise as per the hypothetical case explained above. As it is almost impossible to know the absolute level of welfare, an absolute optimal can't be achieved in practice. Presumably, an absolute optimal is not necessary either as businesses usually operate based on the continuous improvement approach rather than an all-embracing optimization at a point in time.

"Experience scorecard" is the newest holy grail

The closest approximation to customer welfare would be a multidimensional scorecard that covers all the critical aspects of the extended product: performance, price, packaging, quality, service and communication. Developing a practically implementable "experience scorecard" with strong predictive supremacy (for customer loyalty and advocacy) is the newest holy grail of practitioners. Many scorecards are available in the industry today: Sapient's ROX (Return on Experience), Forrester's CXi (Customer Experience Index) and Temkin's TxR (Total Experience Rating) are probably the best-known metrics. These metrics rate customer interactions based on criteria such as success, ease, quality, consistency and emotional connection. Although developing a multicriteria scorecard is a reasonable approach, none of these experience ratings are well-established or credible enough to become a global reference yet.

Despite their unidimensional nature (i.e. measuring a specific aspect of interaction) and consequent inadequacy, three simple indicators – Net Promoter Score (NPS), Customer Satisfaction (CSAT) and Customer Effort Score (CES) – are the most frequently used metrics in the area of customer experience management.

Table 6. Mapping of customer experience indicators

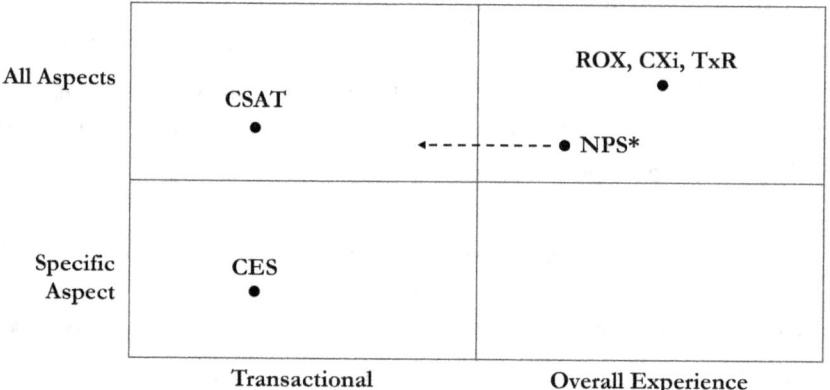

* NPS becomes a transactional indicator if the customer is surveyed right after a specific interaction

Let's revisit NPS, CSAT and CES with the aim of understanding what they actually imply and how they can be used in practice.

Table 7. Comparison of NPS, CSAT and CES

	NPS	CSAT	CES
Definition	Likelihood of a customer recommending a product	Level of customer satisfaction from an interaction	Level of effort levied on the customers in an interaction (such as, while handling a request)
Question	"How likely are you to recommend the product to a friend or colleague?"	"How satisfied are you with the retail/ service/ website experience?"	"To what extent do you agree on the following statement: The brand made it easy for me to handle my issue"
Scale	A scale of 11, where 10 means "extremely likely" and 0 means "not likely at all"	Commonly a scale of 5, where 5 means "very satisfied" and 1 means "dissatisfied"	Commonly a scale of 7, where 7 means "strongly agree" and 1 means "strongly disagree"

Calculation	Respondents are segmented into three groups: Detractors (rating from 0 to 6), Passives (rating 7 or 8), Promoters (rating 9 or 10) NPS is the difference between the proportion of Promoters and Detractors in the sample: NPS = (Number of Promoters – Number of Detractors) / Sample Size	Respondents rating 4 and 5 are classified as "satisfied" CSAT is the percentage of satisfied customers in the sample: CSAT = (Number of customers rating 4 and 5) / Sample Size	Average rating CES = (Sum of all responses) / Sample Size Note: the higher the score, the lower the effort as the question is about "easiness." This is more intuitive than the alternative version which questions "the level of effort" (i.e. the lower, the better)
Range	-100 to +100	0% to 100%	1 to 7

Popularity	Commonly tracked; most respected metric by executives	Most traditional metric; losing its popularity to the newer indicators (NPS and CES)	Most recently invented indicator; becoming increasingly popular

Net Promoter Score (NPS)

Now, let's review these indicators in a bit more detail, starting with the most controversial metric: NPS. Based on my experience, it is a useful but overrated indicator. It is frequently quoted as a miracle metric: the best predictor of growth and the only loyalty metric (!) that companies need to improve in order to grow their business. Moreover, it is claimed that each executive should know it by heart and track it closely. These overstatements and a score of blind followers (amazed by the simplicity of a supreme number that summarizes it all) have made NPS one of the most popular business metrics (at the expense of CSAT) since it was introduced by Frederick Reichheld in 2003. Some companies make NPS part of the strategic objectives and reviews and even tie the executive compensation to its progression. Many businesses implement companywide NPS improvement initiatives. There lies the issue, because it is not as powerful as they believe. Moreover, NPS measures advocacy, but not loyalty.

The predictive capability of NPS and its supremacy over other measures is a long-debated subject. Under certain conditions, some researchers demonstrated that companies with a higher NPS deliver better revenue growth compared to companies with a lower NPS. However, other researchers demonstrated that CSAT and other loyalty measures (such as the likelihood of a repeat purchase) are comparable to NPS, if not better, at predicting business performance. Establishing a causal relationship between the NPS and revenue growth is tricky. Even if we assume that there is a strong correlation between the two in some industries, it could be the case that another variable (such as CSAT or a yet-to-be-discovered measure) is the driver of both NPS and revenue (a phenomenon called "omitted variable bias" in statistics).

Leaving aside the questionable predictive capability of NPS, it is unquestionably a poorly constructed measure. It assigns importance to the high end of a scale (rating 9 and 10), but pretty much ignores the low end (rating 0 and 1). It assumes a customer rating 6 has the same dislike towards the product as a customer rating 0. More importantly, the question is based on the likelihood of recommendation: it has no reference to disparagement. A customer who is unlikely to recommend will not necessarily disparage. Actually, it is pretty unlikely that a customer rating 6 (a detractor according to the NPS methodology)

would ever disparage and, in any case, rating 0 (also a detractor) indicates a more militant and potentially active behavior than rating 6. Rating 0 is the equivalent of showing someone the finger and shouting out loud: "you deserve nothing."

Think about this extreme case: two companies ask a hundred customers about their likelihood to recommend their products. One company receives a hundred sixes. The other company receives one seven and ninety-nine zeros. Which business would you prefer to own? According to the NPS methodology, the second product has a higher NPS (-99) than the first one (-100). Nevertheless, I could not imagine that an executive would prefer to be in charge of the second business. NPS hides the true distribution of the customer responses. An all six rating and an all zero rating produce the same NPS.

You can counterargue that these extreme cases do not exist in real life. That is probably true. However, extreme cases help to make the point more obvious. Less extreme examples could easily be developed to make the same argument: we are tweaking a mathematical formula at the end of the day. The important thing to keep in mind is that customers come in a continuous spectrum: classifying them into three buckets based on a 11-scale measure and clustering more than half of the scale in one "detractor" bucket is not realistic. Extremes of the rating scale are more indicative as we are looking for strong cues of a potential militant behavior (i.e. advocacy or disparagement). Special attention needs to be paid to the size of the bottom two boxes and to the customers marking these boxes.

Advocacy doesn't necessarily imply loyalty (and vice versa)

The broad claim that NPS measures customer loyalty is also far-fetched. It does not measure whether the existing customers will continue to use the product, nor does it measure whether they will use it more or less frequently (or in more or less quantity). It is arguable whether or not a customer who recommends the product will continue to use it: maybe the product no longer meets her needs (or she does not it need it anymore), but she has friends who could be interested in it. It is more accurate to claim that NPS offers a measure of the viral power – or advocacy – of the product. Advocacy does not automatically imply loyalty. Advocacy is an extrovert behavior that aims to influence others, whereas loyalty is an introvert behavior that involves only oneself. You may observe that your most loyal customers are not advocating your product at all. Or vice versa: your fiercest advocates are not necessarily loyal. Take my best friend as an example. He is someone who is interested in technology and electronics. Each time I see him, he has a new smartphone in his hand. When I ask him why he changed phones, he explains how his current smartphone is much better than his previous one. He tells me that he sold his old smartphone on eBay and bought this one. Then he advises me to do the same. This cycle repeats itself every second month. To be honest, the first time, he got me. But then I understood that he is not a genuine advocate: he is just an enthusiast. He has a big personality and he is overly vocal. That is simply who he is. He advocates for the products that he owns, but he is not loyal to them at all.

It is also challenging to set improvement targets using NPS as it strangely ranges from -100 to +100. What level of improvement do you achieve by increasing your NPS from -20 to +20? Improving it from -20 to +20 or from +20 and +60, do these two increases correspond to the same amount of improvement in business results? Any NPS improvement is obviously good; however, an inability to compare one NPS figure to another NPS figure in a quantitative manner renders NPS a less than perfect metric for progressive optimization.

More than its mechanical flaws, the real issue is that NPS is not actionable. It is vague. It neither provides any real insights nor answers the question as to what lies beneath the rating. In order to address this weakness, Reichheld suggested an open-ended follow-up question to explore why customers are not willing to recommend the product.

Actual behavior is a more powerful indicator
than a claimed potential future act

The next obvious question is why would you resort to a claim-based measure for advocacy? Simply ask your new customers their source of product awareness and track the proportion of customers ticking the "I heard it from a friend" box. This is a behavioral measure and much more accurate: actual behavior is more factual than a claim about a future possible act. There is a long path from having the intention to promote a product to actually promoting the product. Are there people around the customer who need such a product? Is the customer a promoting type? Has he been involved in a conversation that triggers a discussion about the product? Recently, I saw a post on LinkedIn about NPS. It was the photoshoot of an NPS survey for Windows 10. The respondent rated the NPS at 0: not at all likely. What is more interesting is the answer given by the respondent to the following "why" question: "I need you to understand that people don't have conversations where they randomly recommend operating systems to one another." We cannot be sure whether this is a real excerpt from a real survey. Nevertheless, I think it illustrates the point well. There could be a tiny little group of customers, ultra-techy people or IT specialists, who may casually chat about Windows. That said, normal people don't. I have even come across NPS surveys on very intimate products, such as feminine washes or lubricants. I am not sure how frequently consumers talk about these products in real life.

NPS could be a useful indicator if interpreted correctly in conjunction with the other measures. Generally speaking, a high NPS (or more customers ticking boxes 9 and 10) is better than a low NPS. There is nothing wrong with a company working to improve its NPS, trying to have a large proportion of potential promoters, as long as NPS isn't turned into a false deity and worshiped.

Customer Satisfaction Score

CSAT is the most conventional measure of customer satisfaction. It is based on directly asking the customer how satisfied he is about a certain touchpoint and episode or the overall experience, depending on the scope defined in the questionnaire. CSAT is an indication of the short-term sentiment (i.e. based on the most recent touchpoint and sentiment at that moment) as opposed to the NPS, which aims to measure the lingering sentiment. Having said that, even if the NPS question is a broad one, the customer response is heavily impacted by the most recent touchpoint. Depending on the nature of the product and inherent complexity of the interactions, companies usually define CSAT targets between 70% and 80%.

The most fundamental challenge with CSAT is what it measures: satisfaction. Although satisfaction is a term frequently used and well understood in business, it is not really meaningful in daily language. We don't usually define our feelings or preferences using the term, satisfaction. We enjoy a dinner. We adore a small seaside town. We appreciate the time we spend with our friends. We like or dislike posts on social media. However, we rarely hear someone saying: "I am satisfied with my vacation." If you heard such a statement, would you take it as a positive or mediocre response? "I'm satisfied" corresponds to rating 4 in a CSAT questionnaire and thereby, contributes positively to the CSAT score. However, in real life, it corresponds more to a rating of 3 than 4. In short, CSAT forces customers to use a business-friendly terminology, which does not correspond to the usual way of classifying human emotions, to define their sentiment. CSAT is more business minded than human minded.

Customer Effort Score

The popularity of CES has been rising since its introduction in a provocative HBR article, "Stop Trying to Delight Your Customers" (Dixon, Freeman, & Toman, 2010). The authors claim that CES has more predictive power than NPS and CSAT for both repurchasing and increased customer spending. The idea behind the metric is that customers punish poor service more than they reward delightful (exceeding expectation) service. The vast majority of care practitioners, including myself, would agree on the underlying idea. However, it is difficult to establish a meaningful connection between this observation and loyalty: that is to say, repurchasing and increased customer spending. In practice, a customer will not continue using a subpar product just because the service offers an effortless experience. CES measures the ease of reactive service delivery; however, for any business, the immediate focus should be on employing preventive and predictive care methods to eliminate the painful interactions from the customer journey.

Customers prefer products that do not fail in the first place. They also prefer products that offer better value for money. They like products with unique design and features. Moreover, the competitive products set the basis of comparison. The loyalty of your customers may evolve over time depending on the competition. In limited-competition markets, customers are loyal despite the fact that service is usually painful because they don't have an alternative to switch to. Ignoring all these factors and claiming that customer effort in reactive service delivery is a predictive indicator of loyalty is, at the very least, an exaggerated statement. Such a claim could only hold true under very specific market conditions. This does not mean that an effortless service experience is not appreciated: it is, presumably more than occasional surprises (such as refunds, discount coupons and free-of-charge service).

In any case, loyalty is a complex, multidimensional phenomenon. Reducing it to one dimension and exaggerating the predictive capability of CES is a strategy which is fundamentally flawed. It is another attempt to find a single miracle metric that is yet to exist. Even if CES doesn't provide insights on what made a transaction easy or difficult (unless asked in a narrow scope, clearly indicating a specific interaction), it is a valuable indicator if used for the right purpose: measuring the most important expectation of the modern-day customer from reactive service delivery. That is to say, making things happen with the simple click of a finger. In this context, easing the interactions that customers expect to be effortful is the most effective way to delight customers. As a practical example, in order to open a bank account, customers need to visit a branch office for identity validation. Customers perceive this to be time consuming and burdensome. Online-only or online-first banks simplify this step by executing the identity validation process remotely through visual communication. Customers would surely rate the effort for opening an account at online-only banks lower than the traditional banks. This simplification surely improves customer acquisition. However, does it really improve loyalty? I wouldn't say so.

CES can be measured for each critical touchpoint throughout the customer journey. For example, you may test the effectiveness of your FAQs: "To what extent do you agree with the following statement: It was easy for me to find answers to my questions by reading the FAQs on the product website." In this narrow use, CES is more specific and actionable than NPS and could be useful in identifying pain points in the customer journey. Moreover, "making it easy" is a more focused goal than "exceeding customer expectations."

CES is directly proportional to First Contact Resolution (FCR) – the percentage of customer incidents resolved fully at the end of the first point of contact, regardless of the channel and eliminating the need for a follow-up communication or reopening. Any incident that is only resolved after multiple contacts is taxing for customers. Therefore, businesses should constantly ask themselves the following questions: Are our agents knowledgeable? Are they able to keep up with the speed of technological advancements? Is it easy for our customers to reach the subject matter experts? Are our processes vague and time-consuming? Do we have processes in place that cover a wide range of user cases? Are our systems capable and reliable? It is wise to ask yourself these questions if you want to improve your FCR and subsequently your CES.

Practical use of these metrics

Despite various claims, none of these metrics are strong enough to assess customer loyalty and advocacy, or to predict revenue growth on their own. The literature is full of conflicting findings. There are multiple studies which favor one metric over the other two. However, these studies have been conducted in a specific industry at a specific point in time. At the time of writing, there have been no studies that were able to demonstrate that one metric was stronger than the other two for every industry and at any point in time. This is not surprising given that it is impossible to prove a fact that does not exist. Revenue growth is a function of acquiring new customers and retaining and selling more to the existing customer base. NPS is probably a better leading indicator for new customer acquisition where as CSAT and CES are probably better (but still limited) leading indicators of retention and revenue per customer. All these indicators demystify a piece of the puzzle even if they claim to predict the whole picture. For such a claim to hold true either the indicators would need to be highly correlated or the acquisition and retention would need to be highly correlated. In this case, you would not need all three metrics as one metric is probably enough to predict the other metrics and thereby all facets of revenue growth. The issue is that these cases are, by definition, specific rather than universal. As a result, we will keep hearing research revelations on how superior one metric is to another for a specific case – for a specific industry and at specific point of time. That is fine as long as researchers do not try to generalize by turning a specific case into a universal rule.

Based on my experiences, I can share the following observations on the practical use of these metrics:

- The measured difference between NPS and other satisfaction measures can be revealing. NPS relates to the overall experience whereas CSAT relates mainly to the service component. If CSAT is consistently high (above 80%), whereas NPS is consistently low (below 20), then you are probably facing enduring product performance issues. In the opposite case, you probably have a subpar service offer.

- Time elapsed between the touchpoint and survey is critical. CSAT and CES are intended to measure the quality of a specific touchpoint. Therefore, the satisfaction survey should immediately follow the completion of the interaction when the customer's memories and feelings are fresh. This will ensure that another touchpoint does not come into play before measuring the quality of the touchpoint that you intending to evaluate. The best practice is making the inquiry in the same channel as the interaction, immediately after the completion of the interaction. Conversely, NPS is a reading of general sentiment. It is important to randomize the timing of the NPS measurement. It should not follow a specific touchpoint. Otherwise, rather than measuring the general sentiment, NPS will measure the quality of that specific touchpoint. Regardless of the wording of the NPS question, respondents will take it as an inquiry to the quality of the most recent interaction. Therefore, including NPS in post-interaction surveys will result in biased results and will not serve the intended used of the metric. NPS is better measured through periodical surveys. Alternatively, your website or app can feature links to an NPS survey, allowing customers to fill in the survey at their own convenience.

- Assuming that your service level is good (i.e. you have a respectable CSAT), your post-service surveys are likely to result in a higher NPS than your periodical surveys. Post-service surveys arrive at a moment of happiness, just after solving a customer issue. Periodical surveys arrive at any time; assuming that randomization is in place, periodical surveys should glean unbiased results. Nevertheless, NPS calculated based post-interaction surveys and periodical survey send-outs usually move in the same direction over time and reflect the overall change in customer sentiment to a similar level of accuracy.

- Taking an NPS measurement at the contact center provides an excellent pulse of the market. Think about a contact center processing ten thousand customer requests per day. Assuming a 3-5% response rate, such a contact center would receive three to five hundred post-contact surveys per day (or nine to fifteen thousand per month). This is an excellent source of information, regardless of the inherent bias. When a company is facing a major disruption in the market, such as a failure of its website or a batch of products suffering from quality related issues, you will immediately see a plunge in the NPS ratings that have been collected through post-interaction surveys. On the other hand, if your business launches a successful communication campaign or an interesting promotion, your daily NPS reading will show a positive jump.

- The referral rate is also a function of the competitive environment. You may come across products that are suffering from a low NPS while enjoying high referral rates. This could be the consequence of being the only viable product available on the market or being the best of the worst (i.e. the best in a disastrous class of products)

- Customers with more pronounced feelings tend to complete the surveys more often. This frequently produces a bipolar distribution of ratings. However, that does not necessarily mean that you have a polarizing proposition, i.e. something that is loved by some and hated by others (like most politicians nowadays). For overall rating calculation purposes, the missing neutral mass doesn't make much of a difference as they are generally ignored during scoring.

- The beauty of NPS is that there is an abundance of data across industries and markets. However, we need to be careful. We should take cross-market comparison with a pinch of salt. Cultural differences play a major role in the ratings. Some nations are culturally less inclined to give higher ratings. Other nations tend to show extreme reactions more easily. I remember what our history teacher told us back in the high school: on the first day of the class, he said "10 belongs to God, 9 is mine, students have a chance for an 8." Think about the NPS ratings given by a nation educated under a mentality that sets very high standards for success and preaches that perfection can be aspired to but cannot be achieved. Good luck to any business finding a promoter there.

It is important to highlight two specific points about the previously mentioned indicators:

(1) *Incentives to increase survey participation rates:* Incentivizing customers to participate in satisfaction surveys could superficially increase the satisfaction scores; for example, after customers receive a gift. We have tendency to treat those who gift us kindly. The worst incentive is awarding participation with a chance to win a big prize rather than distributing the same small prize to every participant. Such an award scheme could lead participants to artificially rate the brand even higher, assuming that the big prize may only be given to a customer who leaves a high rating. If it is absolutely necessary, indirect prizes, such as loyalty program points, should be offered.

(2) *Bias in the sample selection:* In some set-ups, service personnel are involved in every survey sent out. They even decide on whether or not to send out a satisfaction survey after the interaction. Such a practice will result in a preselected sample and biased results, especially if the compensation of service personnel is linked to the measured customer satisfaction score. Whenever possible, the survey should either be randomized by automation or offered to the entire customer population (100% survey send-out without sampling). Moreover, the risk of ser-

vice personnel interfering with the evaluation processes should be eliminated. Here are two personal experiences, both from the auto industry:

- A few years ago, I bought a car from the local dealership of a well-known manufacturer. After completing the transaction, the sales assistant told me that I would be receiving a phone call from their HQ to measure my satisfaction. She also told me that she would appreciate a 5-rating. Later in the day, she called me to check whether everything was all right with my new car and reminded me about the 5-rating. She did the same thing the morning after. I received a short call from their HQ (the contact center of the auto manufacturer) that afternoon. The most dissatisfying side of buying a car from that manufacturer was the persistence concerning the satisfaction survey from the sales assistant.

- My sister had an even worse experience. The sales assistant at her car dealer handed out an NPS survey, already marked 10, for her to sign. When my sister asked them about it, the sales assistant explained that it was just a formality requested by their HQ and it was intended to be a "feel good" exercise where everyone just marks 10.

Obviously, both sales assistants were incentivized based on their rated service delivery and they were trying to influence the ratings. Maybe these are extreme examples; nevertheless, when incentives are in play, be careful about the possible rigging of the results.

Another perspective

Up to now, we have reviewed in depth the three most frequently used metrics in the area of customer experience management: NPS, CSAT and CES. They are all useful indictors if used collectively in the right context and while keeping in mind their respective limitations. However, none of these indicators directly measures the quality of your care practice. A more focused evaluation metric is needed for this purpose.

Care is a fundamental aspect of a brand and the level achieved by a business's care practice can be assessed based on its contribution to the overall brand perception. Which one leads? The perception of the brand in general or the perception of its care practices?

Which one leads? Care or overall brand perception?

One simple question can be added to your periodical customer surveys to evaluate whether you are a care-first business:

On a scale of 5, where 5 means "strongly agree" and 1 means "strongly disagree," to what extent do you agree to the following statement: "What I like most about Brand X is the way it takes care of what I need or want."

We can classify the care practice in four categories based on the average response:

- Failing (rating 1-2): care is perceived to be inferior to the brand, bringing down the overall experience; it is fair to assume that customers frequently feel disappointed and frustrated ("they cannot even take care of the mess they create").

- Functioning (rating 3): somewhat meets the customer expectations, but does not add to the overall experience ("my problems are resolved when I ask").

- Differentiating (rating 4): care presumably generates some loyalty and advocacy for the brand by consistently meeting all customer expectations (wants/needs) and creating surprises by frequently exceeding them ("my problems are resolved even before I ask").

- Disruptive (rating 5): care clearly leads the overall brand image by unearthing unrecognized needs and driving customers' expectations (from a care practice) forward; facilitates the evangelization of the brand among the customers ("I am blessed to have them; I know they have always got my back").

The eventual goal for a practitioner is to build a mental image of a differentiating or disruptive care-first brand in customers' minds. We defined seven guiding principles that will help your business to create an enduring perception of having a caring attitude. The key question is: How do you perform as a business in each of these principles? Ask your customers. The feedback you receive will offer you many eyeopeners and help you identify improvement opportunities.

You may add a section to your periodical customer surveys to evaluate how well you do in each principle:

To what extent do you agree with the following statements?

Table 8. Statements to be used in the evaluation

Statement	Strongly disagree	Disagree	Neither agree nor disagree	Agree	Strongly agree
My interactions with Brand X are simple					
I see Brand X getting better over time					
I think Brand X is a trustworthy brand					
What Brand X offers is always relevant to me					
I care about Brand X					
I think Brand X helps me all the time					
I think Brand X's actions are consistent					

The idea is to identify and take the right actions in order to have more of your customers agreeing with these statements each time you rerun this survey. In the areas in which you perform poorly, you may wish to conduct qualitative research in order to collect insights on why your business is perceived that way, for instance, why your customers think that it is not simple to interact with your business.

Ultimately, no one metric is able to provide all of the information a company needs regarding its customer approval, net promoter, and care-efficacy performance. As we have discussed in this chapter, tracking and quantifying customer delight, loyalty and advocacy comes with myriad pitfalls and shortcomings, which can only be overcome by employing a critical and suspicious eye when evaluating a single metric. We can conclude that the use of multiple metrics at once is likely to provide more meaningful and applicable insights.

CHAPTER 8

Contact Centers
of the Future

We began the book by talking what care is not about. I believe that since then, we have managed to define the broad scope of care such that it extends well beyond the stereotypical image of care consisting only of contact centers. Nevertheless, it would be negligent to finish this book without a short section on the changing face of contact centers, which still form an important point of customer interaction.

Frequently referred to as a call center, a contact center is an operating hub which manages all human-assisted interactions in remote communication channels controlled by a business. These channels include voice call, video call, instant messaging, text message, mail/fax, live chat, e-mail and social media. It is a point of customer contact, a gateway to many channels. Nowadays, contact centers are living a Cinderella story: the maid is turning into a princess. As the scope of activities broaden and the volume of direct customer interactions multiply, contact centers are turning into Centers of Customer Operations (CCO), where the heart of a company beats. With the rise in experience-based brand differentiation, contact centers are becoming the focal point in leading the delivery of a seamless omnichannel experience. They are evolving to be the backbone of the commercial execution capability for any business heavily involved in direct customer interactions.

In today's connected world, businesses increasingly aspire to engage in positive interactions with their customers in order to improve the perception of their brand. The sum of these interactions defines the overall customer experience: what the customer feels, remembers and is likely to pass on to other customers. The pathway to loyalty and advocacy is paved by each and every interaction. Considering that a large proportion of customer interactions take place in remote communication channels managed by contact centers, agents are becoming the embodiment of your brand.

As discussed earlier, contact centers are not only the voice of your brand, they are also the ears. Considering that a large portion of customer interactions take place through contact centers and there is the capability to record and analyze these interactions in full, contact centers should play an important role in developing customer insights.

Contact centers possess the capability to reach out to customers through remote communication channels. This capability enables businesses to quickly pilot ideas or test initial customer interest on different concepts. Considering that businesses are, more than ever, under pressure to develop and test quickly in today's fast-evolving market environment, such a capability is becoming increasingly important.

Contact centers have full access to company resources and customer databases. They are able to record and track all customer interactions. Accordingly, agents are empowered to take proactive actions based on personalized offers.

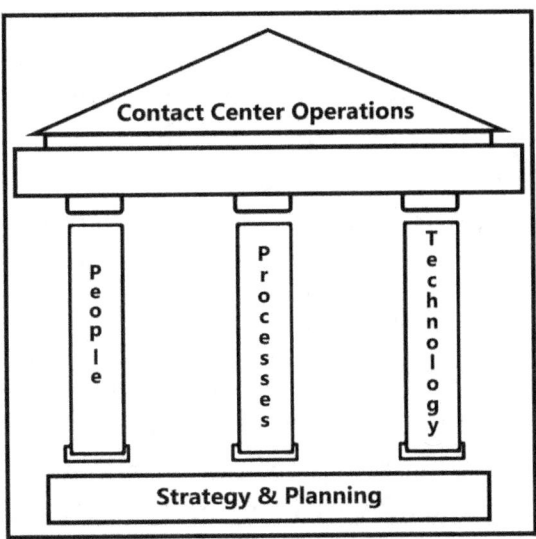

All these benefits render the operational excellence of a contact center more critical for business success. The contact center operations are built on three pillars: processes, technology and people. We will review how these three pillars are evolving hand-in-hand with each other.

Practices & processes

Service diversity is increasing at lightning speed. Service processes are becoming more complicated with multiple alternative flows and endpoints as a result of mass personalization. Face-to-face interactions are decreasing in number, whereas remote interactions – mainly using mobile devices – are skyrocketing in parallel with the advancement in technology. People are more connected than ever before, but remotely. Accordingly, as the center of remote communications, contact centers are increasingly becoming the primary meeting point between customers and businesses and thereby, a make-or-break spot for the onset, improvement and continuity of the relationship. Contact centers are positioned to create more business value rather than focusing on their traditional firefighting role in resolving customer issues. In parallel, the business focus should shift from cutting the cost of an inconsequential activity to maximizing the value created by business-critical activities.

It is no longer about shortening contact handling times

The ultimate objective should be to improve the depth and quality of customer interactions. A contact center is neither a cost center nor a profit center: it is a mix of both, but more importantly, it is a sustainability center. In the future, contact centers will mainly focus on advising customers, complex issue resolution, upselling and cross-selling. The question is how to put in place the right mentality and approach in order to be successful.

As a general trend, the pressure on contact centers to sell through outbound contacts is in decline as telemarketing has been proven to be vastly ineffective. This ineffectiveness is due to the fact that telemarketing creates an army of detractors at the expense of generating only a few new customers. Receiving a cold call from a seller is overly intrusive for customers. Accordingly, voice calls are being increasingly replaced by less intrusive and less costly outreach methods such as outbound e-mail or text message campaigns.

However, there is increasing pressure on contact centers to sell during inbound contacts. If the inbound call is an inquiry about your products, then selling will consequently follow as a natural step in the process. Actually, in this case, selling the right product is a form of helping the customer. However, if the inbound contact is about an issue faced by the customer, then trying to sell something is a counter-productive attempt. If your care practice turns into a pretext to promote your products, your care practice boils down to sales and marketing. Who will your customers trust when there is no impartial party left in your camp? Selling should never be the objective of care. Selling should be the outcome of good care. Care has one overarching objective: building trust. The agents are expected to quickly diagnose and resolve customer problems, identify unvoiced customer needs or wants and develop recommendations or make offers that resonate with these customer needs or wants. As a result of their passion, trust and genuine concern, these are the type of agents that make customers want to buy. With this "sales through care" approach, super-skilled agents will be in high demand.

Technology

Contact center technology is advancing quickly. Through digitalization, contact centers are redefining the customer experience to a level unmatched by any other point of interaction. New technologies are able to deliver both cost reduction and customer satisfaction improvement at the same time by enabling the automatization of data analysis, information search and processing tasks in the contact center. Deployment of these technologies help:

(1) automate repetitive tasks and eliminate mundane agent work. These tasks include retrieving customer interaction history, tagging and categorizing emails, rerouting calls and handling simple customer inquiries (such as processing refunds or tracking shipments).

(2) improve the interaction outcome by recommending cross-selling/upselling offers and pushing personalized content for customer education.

(3) strengthen quality control by detecting customer sentiment, flagging problematic interactions and analyzing agent performance.

(4) identify trending issues or topics in real-time.

We can categorize these technological advancements into three groups: cloud-based connectivity, intelligent Interactive Voice Response (IVR) and speech analytics. Next, we will review each of these groups in more detail.

Cloud based connectivity unifies operations,
while eliminating the need for cohabitation

Global companies typically operate with multiple contact centers and these centers are usually located in different countries. It is critical to have a unified telephony infrastructure in place to manage all inbound and outbound activities. This will allow full flexibility in Business Processes Outsourcing (BPO) partner management as well as centralization of data recording and management. Moreover, customer inquiries can be routed based on previous interactions, purchase history and skill-based teams.

Moreover, cloud-based CRM and unified omnichannel communication platforms enable efficient team collaboration, irrespective of the location of team members. These solutions are a key enabler for the employment of remote service agents. Bringing the contact-handling task to the physical location of the agent, rather than bringing the agent to the contact center, allows businesses to benefit from a more flexible workforce and to scale up and down quickly depending on the demand. Cloud-based solutions provide businesses with an opportunity to break down the silos that could be holding them back and stopping them from offering the services that customers need.

Intelligent IVRs take over the processing of simple tasks in bulk

Customers frequently complain about waiting in the queue, waiting on hold, navigating through a complex IVR system, incompetent agents and the need to talk to multiple people. Intelligent IVRs, powered by AI and NLP (Natural Language Processing), are turning into a powerful platform to resolve customer issues (such as responding to FAQs). It makes better business sense to use IVR in this context instead of some irritating, self-repeating commercial communication such as "Your Brand. The most preferred consumer brand according to the Whatever Magazine" or "Don't forget to sign up for our membership program. A world of benefits is waiting for you."

A customer's identity can now be recognized automatically by methods such as incoming number recognition, voice recognition, biometrics and speech-to-text conversion of the stated identity. Subsequently, intelligent IVR can extract the customer's history and, thanks to the new breed of NPL applications, can engage in a natural dialogue with the customer to understand the root of the inquiry. Thereby, IVR can also provide sorting and (behavior or insights-based) routing assistance by directing the call to the right agent. This reduces customer effort by eliminating the need for customers to listen to multiple IVRs and press numbers to navigate through the phone tree and reach the right agent.

Speech analytics boosts analysis and prediction capabilities

Speech (conversation) analytics solutions are designed to recognize and understand words, context, sentiments or emotions. They could come into action before, during or after a live agent interaction. As mentioned before, customer and issue identification are the main areas of use before the live interaction. In addition, gender, age and the emotional state of the customer could also be recognized before the human-to-human interaction begins; for instance, an obviously upset customer could be routed to a specially-trained agent.

Speech analytics can be used in a predictive manner during live interactions to support agents in developing personalized experiences for customers. Live analytics software automatically analyzes the customer's speech and emotional state by assessing the customer's mood through keyword and tonality detection. Thereby, it provides service personnel with all the highly relevant information they need to deliver quality service as well as suggesting how to improve the customer experience in real time. These capabilities potentially help boost customer satisfaction. Moreover, by analyzing every customer contact and comparing it with thousands of other contacts (in terms of interaction characteristics and predicted/recorded interaction outcome), such software can develop "how to interact" strategies. These strategies range from showing empathy to asking the right questions to expanding a conversation in order to arrive at a product recommendation. Machine Learning (ML) solutions help contact centers provide better quality service and strengthen their cross-selling and upselling activities. Live analytics also raise red flags in the case of a problematic interaction by informing supervisors about situations that require their involvement and intervention. They also enable the display of statistical dashboards and provide real-time overview of customer experience metrics.

Speech analytics after live interactions can extract insights from customer interactions by revealing the most frequently made complaints and the most common reasons why customers contact you. Speech analytics search for opportunities to improve the customer experience by systematically scanning calls to spot and/or predict trends and underlying contact drivers. It demystifies the relationship between different topics and analyzes agent performance. Insights derived from the post-mortem analysis could be used to train both human and digital agents on how to best respond to different inquiries and flows of conversation. While AI helps improve human performance, thanks to its real-time big data analysis capability, human agents help bots learn the more human-sensitive and intuitive responses. Other immediate areas where speech analytics could be used include assessing customer satisfaction on the different dimensions of the business (such as the product, agent, communication, promotional offer) as well as preventing fraud and leakage of sensitive information.

Commonality among the technology-enabled tasks include big data analysis and execution of repetitive procedures. As a result of Robotic Process Automation (RPA,) agent time is made available for the more complex tasks that require human interaction. Inherent capabilities lead to a natural division of duties between humans and machines: that is to say, what is handled by AI, what is handled by humans and what is handled by both in tandem.

People

The aspired benefits of an enabling technology and process can only be realized if the human performance can be improved in parallel. As the number of service applications and the consequent need for multi-tasking increases, agents with more versatile skills will be required to manage the complexity of customer interactions. Having said that, whenever self-service and AI-assisted service solutions fail to resolve cases, escalation will be made to human agents. As more customers adopt self-help and solve their issues on their own, the incoming contacts will be related to more complex matters, including technical issues involving digital self-help solutions.

As agents will be confronted by customers with complex inquiries and probably in a more agitated state of mind, the ideal agent profile will require more advanced technical and interactions skills. Modern agents should also be able to operate across a range of new digital interaction channels. There will be an increase in customers calling just to vent their frustration with the self-service solutions. Modern agents will need to make more difficult decisions on their own. This means that they should be skilled in decision-making and empowered to act. In any case, the key for agents to be successful while interacting with these high-stress customers will be to shift their attitude and increase their aptitude in answering difficult questions.

Operating a contact center is no longer as easy as picking up the phone. With the multiplication of communication channels and reaching out to service from any channel (whichever is more convenient on a given occasion) becoming the norm, service agents should be able to communicate fluently in a multitude of channels. Certain channel-based segmentation is unavoidable. For example, not every agent is up for a video call or live chat. That being said, aspiring agents should be able to handle a few media streams as the customers will increasingly be digital natives who feel comfortable cruising through different channels. An interaction that started with live chat may turn into a phone call, followed by an informative email.

The service agent profile will progressively shift from efficient problem-solvers operating at a robotic tempo to relationship-builders. This doesn't mean that agents won't need problem solving skills in the future. However, they will have more support tools at their disposal to solve problems whereas the core skill that they will need to bring into the mix will be relationship-building. More social and hospitality workers, maybe even caretakers, will be attracted to agent positions.

People try to do what they are incentivized to do. Accordingly, agents should be incentivized based on the depth and quality of the interaction, rather than speed – rather than keeping the sludge moving and having the lines open, as the saying goes.

Businesses should introduce relevant post-interaction questions, such as the depth of interaction or service personalization. For instance, ask your customers: "To what extent do you agree on the following statement: the service personnel went the extra mile (above and beyond) to help me out?"

Virtual contact centers will employ home-based agents and agents at multiple onshore or offshore sites. Future agents should be comfortable in using digital solutions and social media. The work-at-home model will bring in cost-savings and offer a better quality of life for the agents. In addition, it will allow the industry to employ the talent that it cannot employ otherwise. Agents will be trained and tested online. They could even be given Uber-like online profiles where their skills are graded by both monitoring algorithms and customers. Maybe customers will decide on the agent to interact with based on these profiles.

Transformation from contact center agents
to customer experience partners

The contact center industry employs around 10 million people worldwide. Replacement of human assistance with AI-assistance presents a social and ethical dilemma. Over time, all repetitive menial tasks will be handled by robots or digital bots and contact centers are no exception to this trend. Some jobs will be lost, but others will emerge. Today, contact center employees earn at the bottom of the pay scale. The choice to become a contact center agent is not necessarily representative of a career path, but rather a temporary employment. Tomorrow, more skilled and better educated agents will be needed in large quantities as the role of human agents becomes critical in the delivery and continuous improvement of positive customer experiences and in the execution of decisive interactions with current and potential customers. Talented contact center agents will increasingly become valuable resources for which businesses compete. The average agent paycheck, as well as the employment benefits and perks, will improve accordingly in order to attract and retain the best talent. Better days are ahead for the contact center agents who are able to embrace this transformation and become customer experience partners. The changing role of contact centers could make the agent job a more viable and long-term career path for the skilled job seekers of tomorrow.

Outlook

There is a heated debate on the future size of the contact center industry. Will the industry maintain its growth trajectory in the presence of machine solutions? Some enthusiastic technology experts predict that, in the next decade, a large portion of customer interactions will be handled by digital solutions (both self-service and AI-assisted service) without the intervention of human agents, thereby reducing the need for contact centers. The proliferation of digital solutions and their increasing popularity, especially among digital natives, is an undeniable fact. However, this doesn't necessarily mean that the number of interactions handled by human agents will be less than today as:

- greater connectivity and improving access to service will result in the multiplication of interactions. Many previously unvoiced concerns will be voiced and the silent majority will become smaller.

- human agents will act as an escalation, support and control point for self-service and AI-assisted service solutions. When these solutions fail, customers will be redirected to human agents. Moreover, human agents will play a key role in educating customers on digital solutions.

- some customers (especially digital immigrants) are less likely to ever be comfortable adopting and navigating through digital solutions.

- not all tasks are suitable for digital handling. There will be a division of labor between the digital and human. Low-value, transactional interactions will increasingly be handled digitally, whereas human assistance will be reserved for more complex, high-value interactions (such as product advisory, brand experience delivery and cross/upselling) and especially, for outbound contacts.

I expect that the growth in workload will surpass the elimination or simplification of mundane tasks through automated solutions over the next decade. Therefore, the industry size – measured in terms of the number of full-time agents – will continue to deliver a healthy growth. Presumably, the advancements in technology and its diffusion into operations will only match the increased workload at a later stage. Nevertheless, industry turnover – measured in terms of total contact center spending incurred by businesses (in-house and outsourced) – will keep growing in line with the need to employ a more skilled workforce and consequent increase in cost per agent.

The in-housing trend will accelerate

Large businesses typically outsource contact center operations to BPO partners while placing small teams at partner sites to ensure operational excellence and control. Why? Because service operations are traditionally regarded as a noncritical, yet costly activity. BPO partners offer the scale, experience and technology to keep costs under control while executing business processes according to the pre-agreed service level.

However, as contact center activities become more critical to businesses, we observe some large businesses insourcing, at least, a part of their operations. By doing so, companies aim to exercise greater control in service operations while ensuring flexibility and speed-to-improve. This trend keeps your customers closer to you and brings the reality of the daily business into ideation and strategic business discussions. The key question is how the BPOs will be affected by this trend.

More than 70% of contact center costs are the direct cost of agents. If the cost elements linked to agents (such as recruitment and training costs, supervision costs, equipment and space costs) are added in, up to 95% of the costs are associated with the number of agents at a contact center. Under these circumstances, contact center BPOs pass on the cost to their clients and operate on razor thin margins (usually single digit). Being a highly fragmented and typically local business, even the leading players in the industry capture only a low single digit share of the global market. Industry consolidation is unavoidable. Moreover, in parallel to the increasing need to attract, motivate and retain a more skilled workforce, BPOs are expected to add more value to the business and enjoy better operating margins.

Whatever trends we see happening within the contact-center sector in coming years, it is clear that the activity scope, technology and staffing of contact centers are on the move. Contact centers are becoming a more critical component of the core business operations. Given this development, we can expect to see large-scale changes in the operations in such centers, as well as the way in which employees (or AI equivalents) engage with customers. The days of low-skill contact-center employees reading from an unvarying script are likely coming to a close, and the skill level, responsibility, and business impact of human staffers appear to be on the rise.

CONCLUSION

Having explored care and its place in the race for providing better customer experience, it is clear that the former approach to care as a reactive customer service function is unlikely to continue to work well in the future. Indeed, especially through advances in technology, excellent care from the outset is becoming not only a means of standing out in a cluttered marketplace but also a means of satisfying ever-increasing customer expectations. As we have discussed, negative customer experiences are known to be more powerful and damaging to a company's reputation than positive ones. With the growing use of digital platforms as a means of not only contacting businesses but also spreading the word about good or bad businesses and products, we must update our definition and approach to customer care.

We have seen through this book that care expectations and strategies are moving away from their former role as a firefighting activity and toward a role in developing positive customer interactions, in the sense of adding value to your brand. With the adoption of social media and other online platforms, customers are able to get in touch with companies more easily, offer their feedback, and have their ideas validated in a public forum. This development is a double-edged sword: this allows customers to feel a sense of ownership and comradeship with the business, but it also allows bad news to spread quickly and in an uncontrolled way. This is where the evolution of care as a core philosophy of a business comes into its own, and where we see the ideas discussed in this book coming into play. Through an efficient and able infrastructure, with the ability to engage with customers in their preferred channel and more or less in real time, the human-minded business is able to demonstrate end-to-end trust building and genuine care in a way that keeps the customer engaged throughout their experience and leaves them feeling more than just satisfied in their interactions.

The ideas we have discussed in this book are groundbreaking and potentially disruptive. Where previous interpretations of care demonstrate kind of a careless approach toward customers, in that customer service channels only react when the customer is dissatisfied rather than working to prevent irritating and damaging problems, the human-minded approach promotes preventative and predictive care from the first customer interaction to the last. What I have provided here is a reflection on how human-minded care might be put into action in companies, and how that care philosophy might evolve in the future. What is plainly needed is further research and analysis. As with any new philosophy, some of what I have suggested will surely prove over time to be accurate, but some of my predictions may be revealed to have room for further refinement. I would be happy to connect with my readers and discuss how we can further progress the thinking laid down in this book. Two heads are better than one and, together, we are smarter.

There are exciting days to come in the world of care. Ultimately, it will be excellent care that leads future businesses to success, as care-first businesses will surely develop better products, more meaningful engagement opportunities and greater customer loyalty and advocacy as a result of their foresight and proactivity.

REFERENCES

American Express. (2017). *Global Customer Service Barometer.*

Cohn & Wolfe. (2017). *The Global Authentic 100.*

Dixon, M., Freeman, K., & Toman, N. (2010). Stop Trying to Delight Your Customers. *Harvard Business Review.*

Fürst, A. T. (2015). The neuropeptide oxytocin modulates consumer brand relationships. *Nature. Scientific Reports*, Volume 5, Article number 14960.

Gallo, A. (2014). *The Value of Keeping the Right Customers.* Harvard Business Review.

McCollough, M., & Bharadwaj, S. (1992). The recovery paradox: An examination of consumer satisfaction in relation to disconfirmation, service quality, and attribution based theories. *Marketing Theory and Applications, Volume: 65.*

Netflix. (2013). *House of Cards (Season 1, Chapter 7).*

Nielsen. (2015). *Global Trust in Advertising.*

Siegel+Gale. (2018). *World's Simplest Brands 2018-2019.*